COLLATERAL DAMAGE

COLLATERAL DAMAGE

THE HUMANITARIAN
CONSEQUENCES OF
U.S. SANCTIONS ON IRAN

KRISTY C. LAM

NEW DEGREE PRESS

COPYRIGHT © 2020 KRISTY C. LAM

COLLATERAL DAMAGE

ISBN   978-1-63676-595-2 *Paperback*
        978-1-63676-235-7 *Kindle Ebook*
        978-1-63676-236-4 *Ebook*

To My Loving Family,
Mom, Dad, Marco, Jojo.

To my friends who've been with me
throughout this process, and my
travel buddies without whom I would
not have had this experience.

This book is for you.

CONTENTS

———

INTRODUCTION   1

PART I   **9**

CHAPTER 1.   HOW WE GOT HERE AND PRECONCEPTIONS   11

CHAPTER 2.   WHAT ARE SANCTIONS?   35

PART II   **61**

CHAPTER 3.   SANCTIONS' EFFECTS ON THE ECONOMY   63

CHAPTER 4.   HEALTH   81

CHAPTER 5.   FOOD   95

CHAPTER 6.   ENVIRONMENT   107

CHAPTER 7.   HOUSING   125

CHAPTER 8.   EDUCATION   133

PART III   **153**

CHAPTER 9.   ARTS   155

CHAPTER 10. CONCLUSION   171

ACKNOWLEDGEMENTS   179

APPENDIX   181

INTRODUCTION

———

"Just three US dollars for a gram?" D, this twenty-something-year-old, wearing glasses and a button-down shirt, asked me with urgency in his voice. We had struck up a conversation by the fountains of Naqsh-e-Jahan Square in Isfahan, Iran. Now a UNESCO (United Nations Educational, Scientific and Cultural Organization) World Heritage site, the Square is surrounded by symmetrical rows of inset arches on each of the four lengths. Though the Grand Bazaar, palace, and mosque embedded in the enclosure all date back to the seventeenth century, many locals can be found regularly congregating in the marketplace or sitting on a bench by the manicured green lawn that lines the inside of the Square.

D was a recent college graduate who studied engineering in college and had an interest in learning languages—which I learned by conversing with him in Mandarin. He hoped to save up enough money to live abroad, perhaps somewhere in Europe, where he envisioned a better future and more employment opportunities than in Iran. To finance his dreams, he had decided to trade saffron—stocking up on kilograms of the valuable, bright red spice with the intention of selling small batches to tourists visiting Iran. Little did D know that the United States would abruptly pull out of the Iran Deal. With expectations of growing inflation and fewer visitors to the country due to worsening foreign relations, D's business idea started to turn sour. He was left with bags of high-quality saffron with no buyers. At $3 per gram, this was less than half the price of the spice in foreign countries. In America, the equivalent quality of saffron could be sold for as much as $8.29 per gram.[1]

D and I were the same age, shared similar interests, and both had ambitious futures. Yet, his country's tumultuous economy had not only cost him his business idea, but the fraught US-Iran relations that were responsible for the sudden economic downturn were also affecting his life plans. His hopes for emigration were all but gone. For now, he was struggling with everyday finances. Standing opposite him, this situation seemed surreal.

As I traveled throughout Iran, I met more and more people like him: people who had taken big risks in their life but lost the optimism that had originally motivated them. Idealism became a luxury when faced with the reality of Iran's volatile economic situation. Young graduates started businesses, but did so knowing that their fledgling companies could collapse within a news cycle. Petroleum engineers became tour guides. People turned to any kind of employment for a viable income, only to learn about the sanctions' wide-reaching impacts.

Yet, despite the myriad stressors arising from the economic burdens and uncertainties, Iranians were patient and generous to locals and foreigners alike. A taxi driver drove up

---

1   "The World's Priciest Foods—Saffron," *CNN Money*, July 23, 2008.

to another car just to warn the owner of some problems with the exhaust pipe. A man offered a packet of gum in his pocket to the young boy in the bazaar begging for food. Everywhere my friends and I went, people gave us their phone numbers in case of any emergencies: "So long as you are in Iran, call me if you ever need anything," they said.

To our surprise, some Iranians were not shy about discussing politics in public. People were unafraid to make fun of the foreign media's portrayal of Iran's religiosity. Many complained about the regime. Some students even openly mocked mullahs (religious clerics) on the street. When asked about countries like the US, where both governments are mutually antagonistic, locals asserted the distinction between their objection towards the US government and their recognition of humanity in the American people.

From my brief three weeks traveling from the north to the south of Iran, I was already impressed by the country's complexity and diversity. Everything from food to religiosity varies from region to region, and within regions. Iranians are generous, proud, polite, modest, brave. They are law-abiding and rebellious. They have a rich cultural history that values art and literature and science. They dislike America, but like Americans. They have so much potential but, in some way or another, they are all held back.

One of the largest hurdles toward seeing Iranians as humans—with hopes, dreams, and rich culture—is the negative public view of Iran as a country and regime. Whereas the regime's actions have been depicted as a religious extremist threat towards international security, Iran's experience of imperialist interference and US meddling throughout history instead suggests a more desperate, defensive view of its actions. Regardless of Iran's real motivations, vilification of the country persists as public perception remains negative. Eighty-eight percent of Americans surveyed in a 2020 Gallup Poll indicated they had "mostly unfavorable" or "very unfavorable" views on Iran.[2] With less than 1 percent of total visitors to Iran from 2014-2018 coming from the US, the general public American discourse on Iran is mostly fueled by the echo-chamber of news media.[3] The combination of the overwhelming antagonism and the lack of American travelers to Iran reveals an absence of understanding and nuance in the public debate.

Following the announcement of the US reimposition of pre-Iran Deal sanctions, Trump posted an image of himself with the words "Sanctions are Coming," playing on a popular phrase from the television series *Game of Thrones*.[4] Polling results suggest the majority of Americans believe sanctions to be "an effective way to… change policies that the United States does not approve of" in general. And more specifically, people "strongly supported" imposing sanctions on Iran as a means of counterterrorism.[5, 6] Yet relative to hostile rhetoric against Iran, there has generally been little coverage about the harms that sanctions inflict on the Iranian people.

While human rights violations are inexcusable, America's sanctions on Iran to "hold the Iranian regime accountable for

2   "Iran 'launches Military Satellite into Orbit' amid Tensions with US," *AP News*, accessed October 21, 2020.

3   "Iran, Islamic Republic Of: Country-Specific: Arrivals of Non-Resident Visitors at National Borders, by Nationality 2014-2018 (07.2019)," *UNWTO World Tourism Organization*, October 16, 2019.

4   Donald Trump (@realDonaldTrump), Twitter, November 2, 2018, 11:01 a.m.

5   "Voters See Economic Sanctions As An Effective Response," *Rasmussen Reports*, July 26, 2017.

6   Megan Reiss, "Americans Support Sanctions … Most of the Time," *Lawfare*, January 22, 2018.

its human rights violations" are hypocritical. These sanctions are implemented as the United States strengthens alliances with Saudi Arabia: a country that scores a 7 out of 100 ("not free") in Freedom House's Freedom in the World 2020 report, maintains repressions on women's rights, migrant rights, and restricts free expression, association, and assembly.[7, 8] Moreover, the comprehensive sanctions regime that the US imposes on Iran in itself violates many rights of Iranian citizens, particularly the right to an adequate standard of living as articulated in the Universal Declaration of Human Rights.[9] As will be explained in the chapters of this book, sanctions impede Iranians' access to healthcare, food, housing, and education, among other rights.

For people fortunate enough to not have experienced the devastating impacts of sanctions and regimes, we have had the privilege of remaining oblivious to their real consequences. When I participated in Model United Nations in middle and high school, my friends and I would throw around the word "sanctions" for dramatic effect, freely and jokingly, as a means of threatening delegates from any country outside our circle of alliances. From a simple Google search of "sanctions memes Model UN," this attitude towards sanctions is not uncommon. Thus, when sanctions frequently came up during conversations with Iranian locals as a major reason for their pessimism, I was struck by how many people were feeling the real consequences of a policy tool that had previously felt like an abstract concept to me.

---

7   "Saudi Arabia 2019," Amnesty International, accessed October 21, 2020.
8   "Saudi Arabia," Freedom House, accessed October 21, 2020.
9   "Universal Declaration of Human Rights," United Nations, October 6, 2015.

Traveling to Iran changed my perception of international relations and foreign policy. I hope that by focusing on the humanity of those who live in Iran, readers will be able to glean the talent, resilience, and kindness of a people so often misunderstood and misrepresented. By highlighting the humanitarian consequences of sanctions in Iran, I hope to pressure current and future policymakers to reconsider the way they levy sanctions. Painting Iran as "the enemy," conflating the Iranian regime with its people, and oversimplifying the consequences of sanctions is unproductive to our understanding of the world, particularly as it becomes increasingly interconnected. Viewing Iran and Iranian people with less hostility, but rather as a source of potential careful collaboration would permit a greater variety of policy options for the United States and encourage more creative and persistent diplomatic efforts to renew US-Iran relations. Isolation leaves all parties worse off: Iranian people suffer unnecessarily, and people from the rest of the world lose access to a source of history, culture, knowledge, and humanity.

Although this book covers sanctions' effects on many essential human needs such as food, housing, health, education, and a sustainable natural environment, there are many equally important topics that this book does not include, such as women's rights, children's rights, refugee rights, mental health, and domestic Iranian politics. Nevertheless, these subjects—and particularly how sanctions may have influenced these dynamics in Iran—are worthy of in-depth exploration in the future.

This book was written primarily to address a young, American audience. It is suitable for students and aspiring policymakers with particular interests in international politics and human rights. It would also be an interesting read for those who would like to develop a better understanding of Iran.

Regardless of any existing interests in the country, understanding Iran as a regional power in the Middle East is essential to developing a global perspective. People in Western societies can benefit from learning about life in an Islamic country with certain rules and guidelines that may seem unfamiliar. Rarely, if ever, do countries in the West experience the everyday consequences of comprehensive economic sanctions, as more often they are the actors responsible for putting them in place. Learning about the context in which Iranian people live is not only a good starting place to broaden our conception of humanity, but also to realize the commonalities between Iran and the West is instrumental to the development of more humane policy strategies. Furthermore, a proper evaluation of the consequences of policy tools is critical to realigning US foreign policy to core American values such as life, freedom, and the pursuit of happiness. Rethinking American policies—such as in the case of Iran— is especially timely, as the Western model of liberalism and representative government is no longer admired by people in many countries as the ideal form of government.

By providing a glimpse into the lives of Iranians, this book aims to shed light on the ordinary people who have become casualties in a political battle between Iran and the US. I hope that humanizing a population that is often overlooked or misunderstood by the West and highlighting some of the impacts that sanctions have had on these people would help bring them to the forefront of foreign policy decision-making. *To what extent is the sacrifice of Iranian lives worth it in the attempt to influence the regime's policies?*

Part I of the book will provide an overview of Iran and sanctions. Part II will discuss how sanctions have affected Iran's economy and impacted the basic rights of Iranian people in relation to healthcare, food, the environment, housing, and education. In Part III, this book will examine the potential for a mutually beneficial exchange between Iran and the international community through the lens of Iran's art scene. Finally, the conclusion will summarize the impacts of sanctions on the Iranian people and provide suggestions for the general public and policymakers to improve human rights conditions in Iran.

Throughout this book, some names are changed or withheld for anonymity.

PART I

CHAPTER 1

HOW WE GOT HERE AND PRECONCEPTIONS

———

Perceptions

Roughly 2,500 years ago, gold and silver, jewelry, animals, and weapons were brought from all corners of the Persian Empire to the city of Persepolis during the Achaemenid dynasty. Sculptural reliefs by the entrance of the Apadana, a reception hall for the king, depicted trade delegations from Syria, Ethiopia, India, and twenty other countries that made up the Empire.[10] Some of the dignitaries were holding hands or touching the shoulders of their companion. The illustration of this peaceful procession is "among the rarest and most pleasant depictions of court ceremonies of the ancient world."[11]

---

10 "Persepolis and Ancient Iran: The Apadana," Oriental Institute at The University of Chicago, accessed October 21, 2020.

11 "Persepolis," *Encyclopaedia Iranica*, last modified August 15, 2009.

Compared to these carvings, modern-day Iran may seem to inhabit an entirely different world. Not only does it have turbulent relationships with its neighboring countries—having been involved in wars and proxy wars in the Middle East—but it has also lost its status as a global power.[12] By using non-state actors, Iran has provided training and financial support to Shia forces and rebel groups. The state has assisted the Assad regime in Syria, advanced missile production capabilities for militias in Iraq, and aided the Houthis in the war in Yemen against Saudi Arabia.[13] A 2013 Pew Research Center study showed that most people in most of the countries surveyed had an unfavorable view of Iran. Beyond the US, where about seven out of ten people had a negative view of the country, people in western Europe and even Muslim countries also had a predominantly unfavorable opinion of Iran.[14]

Where Did These Perceptions Come From?

The breakdown of Iran's foreign relations can be primarily attributed to a series of events involving the United States. Many Iranians still blame the US for CIA involvement in the 1953 coup, whereby the popular Prime Minister Mohammad Mosaddegh—who nationalized British-held portions of Iran's oil industry—died under house arrest.[15] For context,

---

12 History.com Editors, "Persian Empire," HISTORY, September 30, 2019.

13 Seth G. Jones, "War by Proxy: Iran's Growing Footprint in the Middle East," Center For Strategic & International Studies (CSIS), March 11, 2019.

14 "Global Views of Iran Overwhelmingly Negative," *Pew Research Center: Global Attitudes & Trends* (blog), June 11, 2013, 154.

15 Abbas Maleki and John Tirman, eds., *U.S.-Iran Misperceptions: A Dialogue*, 1st ed. (Bloomsbury, 2014), 154.

Mosaddegh and Mohammad Reza Shah (the Iranian monarch) were in a struggle for control over the government. The US supported the Shah, who had implemented reforms to modernize Iran as a secular society. The CIA sponsored newspaper articles against Mosaddegh, and Kermit Roosevelt Jr (grandson of Theodore Roosevelt) had coordinated Operation Ajax as a coup attempt to overthrow the Prime Minister.[16]

The Shah was unpopular among the lower classes, the Shia clergy, merchants, and students. Besides instituting pro-western policies, the autocratic Shah had made unfavorable decisions such as repressing political dissent and distributing the country's oil wealth unequally. Domestic discontent combined with a conservative clergy conspiring to oppose an Iranian democracy led to the Iranian revolution in the 1970s.[17] The Shah was overthrown, and the new regime declared itself the Islamic Republic. Many of the Shah-era reforms were reversed and the gradual re-Islamization ensued.[18] Towards the end of the revolution, the deposed Shah was admitted to the US for medical treatment. In the midst of revolutionary fervor, some radical students occupied the US embassy in Tehran in late 1979, demanding the Shah's return to Iran to stand trial for crimes committed.[19]

Although these students may have originally intended to stage a temporary protest for a few hours or days, the act

---

16   Axworthy, *Revolutionary Iran*, 50.

17   Ramtin Arablouei and Rund Abdelfatah, "Four Days In August," July 11, 2019, in *Throughline*, podcast, 38:00.

18   Azadeh Niknam, "The Islamization of Law in Iran: A Time of Disenchantment," Middle East Research and Information Project (MERIP), Fall 1999.

19   "Mohammad Mosaddegh," *Encyclopædia Britannica*, accessed October 21, 2020.

heightened domestic political tensions and devolved into a multi-year affair that caused an international crisis.[20] Iran had violated diplomatic codes of conduct by taking over a foreign embassy and refusing to release hostages. The country, being "anti-American and highly aggressive," became a serious threat to US national interests.[21] By April 7, 1980, the US formally severed diplomatic relations with Iran, which have not been restored since.[22] Meanwhile, the American public—for 444 days—watched on television a "daily barrage" of coverage on the crisis, solidifying their impression of Iran's "fanatical hatred" towards the United States.[23]

Three Prevailing Perceptions

Since then, Iran has become increasingly isolated from the global community as perceptions of the country have worsened. US antagonism towards Iran in the twenty-first century can primarily be characterized in three ways: "Iran the evil theocracy," "Iran the rogue," and "Iran the nuclear menace."[24]

The US perceives the conservative, religious nature of the Iranian regime to be "*inherently* opposed to American values and interests."[25] Iran's foreign policies, especially its desire to expand its regional influence, are perceived as a threat to the US and its allies. Iran, led by an unpredictable regime

---

20 Axworthy, *Revolutionary Iran*, 50.
21 Ibid, 58.
22 Suzanne Maloney and Keian Razipour, "The Iranian Revolution—A Timeline of Events," Brookings Institution, January 24, 2019.
23 Axworthy, *Revolutionary Iran*, 58.
24 Maleki and Tirman, eds., *Misperceptions*, 60-77.
25 Ibid.

motivated by religious ideology, would be even harder to control if it developed nuclear capabilities. Yet, the US remains allies with similarly undemocratic, Islamic regimes in the Middle East despite American "values."

There have been instances of collaboration between the US and Iran when their interests have aligned—such as when the Iranian Revolutionary Guard Corps (IRGC) and the United States worked "closely together" to form Afghanistan's government in 2001, or when the Iranian government "forcefully condemned" the 9/11 attacks—both of which occurred shortly before (much to Iran's surprise) Bush denounced Iran in his "Axis of Evil" speech.[26] While hostile rhetoric may have been used by both sides, Iran's current Supreme Leader, Ali Khamenei, has "never in practical terms taken any steps to jeopardize the survival of the system by triggering a military conflict with the US or Israel."[27] Moreover, retaliatory policies are methodical and defensive—such as in the aftermath of the assassination of General Qassem Soleimani, whereby Iran's actions were described as "strategic revenge" against America.[28] Regarding the country's support for proxies in the Middle East, one local offers an interesting justification from the perspective of Iranian self-defense: "Of course the Iranian government doesn't have the power to fight against the US government. But what they can do is make a mess in other countries," he told me.

Moreover, Iran's nuclear program may, in reality, be more of a rational, pragmatic development based on political

---

26 Mohammed Harun Arsalai and Wil Patrick, "Iran's Shifting Afghan Alliances Don't Fit Easy Narratives," February 18, 2020.

27 Shahir Shahidsaless, "For Iran, Retaliation Is More than a Matter of Saving Face," *Middle East Eye*, January 8, 2020.

28 Ibid.

calculations rather than something ideological or fanatical that "might not be deterrable."[29] Under current President Rouhani, Iran had been compliant with conditions of the nuclear deal for three years until the US withdrew from the agreement in 2018. Even then, Iran has been "notably measured in building up its nuclear capabilities," suggesting the regime's behavior to be relatively predictable and driven by politics, rather than ideology.[30]

Popular preconceptions of Iran may therefore stem from a misrepresentation of the country's motivation. Portraying Iran as an irrational, extremist regime that is the enemy of America leads to a host of negative consequences. Not only does it negatively affect the lives of ordinary Iranians (as will be elaborated in the rest of this book), it also limits the range of possible policy options for US policymakers if their decisions are based on a fixed and inaccurate set of assumptions.[31]

In the Media

For most Americans, their understanding of Iran can be generally attributed to the media as a result of difficulties in obtaining first-hand information. Barriers such as travel restrictions and sanctions limit the extent of interaction and collaboration between people in the two countries. Basing perceptions on news reports that highlight the regime's aggression perpetuates antagonism, reinforces the

---

29 Maleki and Tirman, eds., *Misperceptions*, 60-77.
30 Richard Stone, "New Tensions Dim Hopes for Salvaging Iran Nuclear Deal," *Science*, June 17, 2020.
31 Jo-Anne Hart, "Perceptions and Courses of Actions toward Iran," *Military Review* 85, no. 14 (October 2005).

above-mentioned preconceptions, and establishes an over-simplified understanding of Iran and the Iranian people. A cursory search on the websites of top US news sources such as CNN, MSNBC, and Fox News reveals article titles such as "Iran attacks bases housing US troops," "Iran will remember what the United States did," and "Pompeo accuses Iran of echoing 'Hitler's call for genocide' over 'final solution' rhetoric," respectively.[32, 33, 34]

Yet, for both the American public and American academics, perceptions significantly change after visiting Iran. "Contradictions between my initial expectations and my firsthand experience in going to and participating in the conference [in Iran] made me aware that I carried a number of unconscious, unquestioned presumptions as a result of simply growing up and living in the West," wrote Professor Peter Horsfield in the Journal of Media and Religion.[35] Due to the nature of information about Iran that Americans receive, many have acquired a relatively one-sided depiction of the country. The predominately antagonistic mainstream understanding of Iran and lack of direct contact fuels polarization between the two countries on both societal and policy-making levels.

---

32 Meg Wagner et al., "Iran Attacks Bases Housing US Troops," *CNN*, January 9, 2020.

33 *Chris Matthews: Iran Will Remember What the United States Did (MSNBC, 2020)*

34 Tyler Olson, "Pompeo Accuses Iran of Echoing 'Hitler's Call for Genocide' over 'Final Solution' Rhetoric," *Fox News*, May 22, 2020.

35 Ehsan Shahghasemi, D. Ray Heisey, and Goudarz Mirani, "How Do Iranians and U.S. Citizens Perceive Each Other: A Systematic Review," *Journal of Intercultural Communication*, no. 27 (November 2011).

Iran Overview

Iran remains the seventeenth largest country in the world and holds many natural resources. Not only does it control the fourth-largest proven oil reserve and second-largest gas reserve in the world, it also contains an abundance of coal, chromium, copper, iron ore, lead, manganese, zinc, and sulfur.[36, 37] These resources provide a significant source of potential wealth. In 2016, around the time the Iran Deal provided sanctions relief, Iran was ranked the second-largest economy in the Middle East and North African region, behind Saudi Arabia.[38]

Taarof

Iranian people are warm, and "genuinely courteous"—to the extent that it may be difficult to discern sincere invitations from polite gestures.[39] There is a strong cultural emphasis on respect, whether within the family unit or towards strangers.

The Farsi word *taarof* describes Iranian etiquette: the manner through which people show deference and gratitude towards others. Meanings are often derived from actions; what is desired may be unsaid—sometimes even the opposite may be spoken. Insisting on paying for the bill or offering to share food are some instances of taarof. Other situations

36 "Iran Oil: New Field with 53bn Barrels Found—Rouhani," *BBC News*, November 10, 2019, sec. Middle East.

37 "The World Factbook—Middle East: Iran," Central Intelligence Agency, accessed October 21, 2020.

38 "Islamic Republic of Iran," World Bank, accessed October 21, 2020.

39 Julihana Valle, "The Persian Art of Etiquette," *BBC Travel*, November 14, 2016.

may be more complex, such as taxi drivers refusing to accept payment the first couple of times it is offered. "You can ask people not to taarof," Fatimeh, who had offered to sleep on the floor so her guest could take the bed, said. "It sometimes works, sometimes doesn't—as the request itself may be a form of taarof."[40]

Similar norms exist in other societies, although to varying degrees. Complimenting someone on their dress or telling an acquaintance that "we should catch up some time," without necessarily meaning it, are both examples of taarof found in American society. According to anthropologist Professor William Beeman, by practicing taarof individuals "seek to raise the other person's status and lower their own" and can be understood as a means of momentarily producing social stability by "achiev[ing] equality" in a hierarchical society.[41]

Though sometimes taarof may be merely a gesture of politeness rather than real intention, its cultural importance stems from a society that values generosity, respect for others, and humility. Travelers are familiar with this otherwise under-appreciated side of Iran, and the phrase "Iranian hospitality" is commonly used to describe their experiences in the country—something unlikely to be experienced elsewhere.

"A guest in Iran is like a cherished precious jewel. People will likely put themselves out for you by sharing what they don't have enough of and spending on what they cannot afford—and that's taarof in its purest form," wrote Julihana Valle for the BBC.[42] When I was on the subway in Tehran,

---

40 Ibid.
41 Ibid.
42 Ibid.

a man smiled at us and offered his chewing gum, the only thing he had with him, even though he didn't speak English beyond the three words: "Welcome to Iran."

On our second day, when we were lost looking for the National Museum, a local spent his day off not only guiding us to the museum but also insistently paying for our entrance tickets and explaining each of the Farsi descriptions for the displays we did not understand. Three students spent their day showing us their university and taking my friends and me to lunch at a cafe they frequented. I had never experienced this level of generosity anywhere else.

Iranian kindness towards strangers is not only experienced by foreign travelers. I spoke to Koohyar, a chemical-engineer-turned-tour-guide from the capital city of Tehran, who was hitchhiking with friends in southeast Iran to a region where "people are scared of traveling" due to its proximity to Pakistan. When they were followed by some local motorcyclists, Koohyar was initially fearful of their intentions. Yet when the locals reached Koohyar and his friends, they initiated a conversation and generously offered for the travelers to stay at their house. The latter gratefully declined, to which the locals responded by offering other forms of help. Upon discovering the travelers were looking for wood to make a fire, "one person just jumped on his motorbike and [left]. Ten minutes later, he [came] back with a lot of wood on the motorbike. He took some gas out of his motorbike, [made] a fire for us." The locals even invited Koohyar and his friends to lunch the next day, which was "very nice." According to Koohyar, "this kind of example happens to everybody" when they are in Iran.

Yet, despite the goodwill experienced by locals and travelers, the inability of foreigners to grasp the complexity in

Iranian culture has led to its characterization as "bizarre" and "disorienting."[43, 44] "I have heard many Westerners complain that taarof is symptomatic of a broader Iranian tendency to clothe everything in ambiguity—and to spend an inordinate amount of time doing so," wrote Christopher De Bellaigue in a 2012 issue of *The Atlantic*, who described himself as having been "suckered by taarof."[45]

Accusations of Iranian insincerity as a result of taarof were similarly expressed in a 2014 article from *Public Radio International* titled "The Persian art of declining what you really want and offering what you'll never give could play a role in US-Iran nuclear talks," which warned US politicians about the practice as they prepared to reach a nuclear agreement.[46] These articles not only promote antagonism against Iranian people and oversimplify their culture, they also reveal an intolerance for cultural ambiguity that caters towards perceived Western attitudes. By "min[ing] ... aspects of tarof that Western audiences find amusing, fantastic, bizarre, and at odds with their own communicative norms and values," the above authors "effectively eras[e] a myriad other ways of doing *tarof* as well as the wide variety of moral valences the concept can have for Iranians," wrote Adam Cameron for *The Guardian* on the subject.[47]

---

43 Shirin Jaafari, "The Persian Art of Declining What You Really Want and Offering What You'll Never Give Could Play a Role in US-Iran Nuclear Talks," *The World from PRX*, November 5, 2014.

44 Christopher de Bellaigue, "Talk Like an Iranian," *The Atlantic*, August 22, 2012.

45 Ibid.

46 Jafari, "Persian Art of Declining."

47 Adam Cameron, "The Artful Dodger: Iranian Tarof and Nuclear Negotiations," *The Guardian*, November 20, 2014, sec. World news.

Views of America vs. Americans

Conversely, when I asked locals what they thought about the United States, I was surprised by the moderate responses toward their political enemy. As stated in the Introduction, many expressed their dislike for the US government, but respected Americans as other human beings. Whether it may be because of their lived experiences studying or working in the US, their knack for getting information beyond state-sponsored media (through Instagram or other news websites), idealism, or some combination of other factors, many Iranians' attitudes are far more balanced and even positive towards certain aspects of American society.

"From the things I've heard, I think they're nice and caring people and also... the best tippers in the world," said a tour guide from Isfahan, who had only met one American in person. Many are open to and enjoy American music and television—using shows like *The Simpsons*, as Koohyar did, as a means of practicing English. Others have applied to US universities (although visas have become a major obstacle), or desire "freedoms" that are forbidden in Iran.[48]

The overall perception of the United States is also more dynamic than what is typically captured in mainstream media. Two years after the "Death to America" chants led by President Mahmoud Ahmadinejad in 2007, a World Public Opinion poll showed that of all the Middle Eastern countries, Iran's approval rating for the US was the highest at 51 percent—and higher than in many of America's foreign allies like India or Turkey.[49] Although the ratings have declined

---

48 Christopher Thornton, "The Iran We Don't See: A Tour of the Country Where People Love Americans," *The Atlantic*, June 6, 2012.

49 Ibid.

since then—86 percent unfavorable as of August 2019, the responses nevertheless suggest Iranians' perception of the US to be changeable and highly contingent on US foreign policy.[50]

Within Iran, there are segments of society that tend to be more liberal and embrace Western democratic ideals than others—particularly city dwellers, younger generations (about half of Iran's population is under thirty), and the upper-middle class. This is shown through the protests largely spearheaded by educated student populations of the Green Movement following the apparently rigged re-election of President Ahmadinejad, or in other lesser-known university uprisings such as those in 2019 on Iran's Student Day. During the latter, students from ten universities demonstrated against the brutal government crackdown on nationwide protests in November, one month earlier.[51, 52, 53] "The streets were bloodied, freedom was sacrificed," they chanted.[54] The November protests, sparked by increased fuel prices, had resulted in over 1,000 deaths, 4,000 wounded and 12,000 people detained.[55] The student protestors also objected to the Student Day speaker at Tehran University, Ebrahim Raisi. Currently the Chief Justice of Iran, Raisi was the Conservative opponent to Rouhani in the 2017 presidential elections

---

50   Nancy Gallagher, Ebrahim Mohseni, and Clay Ramsay, "Iranian Public Opinion under 'Maximum Pressure'" (The Center for International and Security Studies at Maryland (CISSM), October 2019).

51   Anthony H. Cordesman, "The Crisis in Iran: What Now?," Center For Strategic & International Studies (CSIS), January 11, 2018.

52   David Patrikarakos, "Analysis: Iran's Younger Generation Positioned To Restore Political Roar," *RadioFreeEurope RadioLiberty (RFE/RL)*, May 18, 2017.

53   Adena Nima, "Iranian Students in 10 Universities Protest Regime's Nov Crackdown," *Iran News Wire*, December 7, 2019.

54   Ibid.

55   Ibid.

and is "despised by Iranians" due to his role in the deaths of over 30,000 political prisoners in 1988.[56]

Alfred, a student visiting Iran on his gap year, recalled some of the conversations he had when he spent a day with a group of university students in Tehran: "The thing that surprised me the most was really just how open they were about their ideas, not so much that they had those ideas—because that was something we already learned was the case," he remarked, referring to the "really radical and revolutionary ideas" these students had on everything from "revolution, [and] Israel" to "the political situation in Iran." In an environment where political dissidents are imprisoned and protestors have been shot down, Alfred was shocked by how much they embraced openness and discussed freely these radical and revolutionary ideas—without much fear of being exposed or thrown in jail.

Alfred added, "I don't know if it was just common courtesy to be polite and not too confrontational about these political issues just to be sensitive... I think definitely some people were aware of that and tried to be a bit careful about not trying to offend or trying to be sensitive, but a lot of people, the overwhelming majority of people I spoke to, were genuinely passionate about being positive towards the United States and the West."

Religion

Besides culture and politics, another oversimplified area of Iranian society often criticized in mainstream western media

---

56   Ibid.

is religion. The Islamic world is generally divided between Shia and Sunni Muslims. While both denominations believe in a singular God and Muhammad as the Prophet, they differ in their belief of leadership following the death of the Prophet Muhammad.[57, 58] Today, the vast majority of people and countries follow the Sunni tradition, while Iran, Iraq, Bahrain, and Azerbaijan are the predominantly Shia countries.[59]

According to James Moore, the "real contemporary [difference]" between the two denominations is "Sunni domination and the oppression of Shi'ites in Muslim countries."[60] The one exception of this case is Iran, where Shi'ism and Sharia Law dominate the country's political, social, and economic aspects and represents a "main threat" to Sunni nations.[61] Because of Iran's minority position relative to other Muslim countries and the "strong antipathy" that many Sunnis feel towards Shi'ites, there is an upper limit to the extent of influence Iran can have in the region.[62]

The Islam that Iran's Islamic Republic practices is not "fundamentalist," but instead adopts many modern innovations rather than calling for a return to earlier and purer forms of Islam, as is the case of Saudi Arabia's Wahhabism.[63]

57 Michael Lipka, "Muslims and Islam: Key Findings in the U.S. and around the World," Pew Research Center (blog), August 9, 2017.

58 John Harney, "How Do Sunni and Shia Islam Differ?," *The New York Times,* January 3, 2016, sec. World.

59 James Moore, "The Sunni and Shia Schism: Religion, Islamic Politics, and Why Americans Need to Know the Differences," *The Social Studies* 106, no. 5 (September 3, 2015): 226-35.

60 Moore, "The Sunni and Shia Schism," 230.

61 Ibid.

62 Mahmoud Eid, "Perceptions about Muslims in Western Societies," in *Re-Imagining the Other,* ed. Mahmoud Eid and Karim H. Karim (New York: Palgrave Macmillan, 2014), 99-119.

63 Ibid.

The "give-and-take" between Iran's complex ancient history and modern society can be most clearly seen by its label as the "nose job capital of the world."[64] Under Sharia Law, women have to cover their hair, arms, and legs (down to the ankles). Yet Iranians' cultural appreciation for beauty, fused with modern medical technology and Islam's standards of modesty, has resulted in the country ranking fourth worldwide in a 2013 study on the number of rhinoplasty operations performed.[65] Ayatollah Khomeini, the founder of the Islamic Republic and then-Supreme Leader, had justified his blessing for nose jobs in the 1980s by quoting "God is beautiful and loves beauty," from the Hadith.[66, 67]

The coexistence of "opposing forces" extends beyond the combination of "rhinoplasty and the roosari" (Farsi term for head-covering).[68] Women can vote, drive, and attend higher education in the same country where murderers must pay the victim's family the price of 1,000 camels or face the death penalty if the family refuses the offer. In cities like Tehran or Shiraz, some women take off their *roosari* in cafes and restaurants. One woman, tired of having to cover herself, even cut her hair boyishly short and wore t-shirts and khakis—and has since gotten away with it, being mistaken for a teenage boy instead. Iranian society exists in the midst of contrasts

---

64 Ryan Cohen, "Rhinoplasty and the Roosari from Ancient Persia to Modern Day Iran," *Hektoen International: A Journal of Medical Humanities,* Summer 2015.

65 "Iran Leaps into World's Top 10 Countries Performing Plastic Surgery," *The National,* January 4, 2016.

66 Rowenna Davis, "Nose No Problem," *New Statesman,* March 6, 2008.

67 Natasha Wynarczyk, "These Persian Girls Are Inciting a National Debate Around Nose Jobs," *Vice,* December 14, 2015.

68 Cohen, "Rhinoplasty and the Roosari."

between old and new rules, freedom and oppression, in a way that is difficult to be captured by any singular representation. When he was still a teenager, Mori had been lashed in public after being caught drunk on the streets of Tehran. Although this technically remains the punishment for alcohol consumption—which is forbidden in Sharia Law—things have since become more relaxed. When "beer" is ordered in restaurants, it only refers to the non-alcoholic kind. But many people have found creative ways to experience intoxication: consuming rubbing alcohol, mixing rubbing alcohol with non-alcoholic beer, adding fermenting chemicals to non-alcoholic beer, brewing home-made alcohol, purchasing it illegally, and so on. Although the lashing was a traumatic experience for Mori at the time, he feels that things have changed. "People are more open-minded now," he said to me. "They know they can't catch everyone… If it were today, the police would not catch me, and the court wouldn't give me lashes. Based on the rules, they still do the same, but they don't catch people for being drunk, really."

Small acts of rebellion have also become commonplace for religious authority figures: "We were walking down the street and saw some mullahs (religious leaders in Islam), who were very recognizable in their garments… and I remember they were walking behind [the mullah] and teasing him," recounted Alfred about the day he had spent with the radical university students, "I don't remember what they did exactly, but they were like, 'oompah loompah,' and walked in a funny way right behind him. It was obvious to everyone around what they were doing, and also to the mullah himself. [The mullah] just walked defiantly—like 'not again' and shaking his head—[as if] it happened a lot of times before… They were making fun of him and making gestures, and making faces, and walking in a funny way—they even said, 'Alfred, you do it too!' which is sort of frightening, since I was a foreigner."

Of course, these depictions do not represent overall Iranian society, nor are university students necessarily all mullah-mocking rebels. When I asked a few female students about whether they feel oppressed as in Iran, they respectfully responded in the negative. Rather, they felt respected. Having a separate subway compartment for women worked in their favor, they said. Even though they could board any section of the subway, the compartments for men tend to be overcrowded relative to the quiet and comfortable front and end portions of the subway, which were generally reserved for women.

An important component of Iran's Islam is the focus on the human condition both in existential terms as well as in interactions between people. Iran has historically played a critical role in establishing the "human and reflective strands of Islamic thought," which have inspired "some of the most profound and beautiful Persian poetry."[69] It demands "decent, honest conduct and the patient endurance of adversity" in its adherents.[70] When asked to describe his religion, Koohyar described it as "beautiful": "All religions say the same thing. It's about being good people, being honest and nice, respecting nature, having discipline…" There is an emphasis on supporting the poor and treating others with compassion and empathy. Koohyar's observance of the religion was on his own terms. He told me, "I was never forced, but it's a part of my culture, so I consider myself a Muslim. But I respect everybody, and I respect other religions."

---

69 Axworthy, *Revolutionary Iran*, xxi.
70 Ibid.

However, due to the "dominant tendency" of negative media depictions of Islam, Muslims are thought of as "a monolith rooted in fanaticism and oppression, portrayed as violent and in clash with 'the West'" overshadows the bases of tolerance, respect, and community found in Islam in general, and especially in the Iranian strand.[71] Contrary to the belief that Iranian Shi'ism is a "dangerous, uncontrollable, fanatical force," Iran's Islam is hierarchical and controlled, guided by senior clerics "most of whom are pragmatic and moderate, and many of whom are out of sympathy with the Islamic regime."[72] For Koohyar, the violence and humanitarianism generated in the name of Islam is not a consequence of the religion, but rather its adherents, "If you give a knife to a crazy guy, he can kill someone, but if you give a knife to a surgeon, he can save a life."

Tensions

In a restaurant across the street from the iconic pyramidal structure known as the Majles—the equivalent of Iran's Parliament—an Iranian friend of mine shouted in exasperation, "Fuck Everything! Fuck Hamas!" We had been talking about politics, and our friend had become exasperated thinking about the amount of foreign aid Iran was giving to non-state actors and terrorist organizations in the Middle East.

In 2019, a state-run Iran Students Polling Agency showed a mere 15 percent satisfaction rating with the performance of the Islamic Republic amongst citizens in Tehran, and more

---

71   Eid, "Perceptions," 100-111.
72   Axworth, *Revolutionary Iran*, xxi.

than half surveyed believe their country's condition is worsening.[73] Although polls conducted within Iran may not be trustworthy, the publicized number remains quite low. Major protests have occurred across the country in recent years. Hundreds of protestors have been killed, and thousands more detained.[74] The November 2019 protests mentioned earlier, which were sparked by a sudden three-fold increase in gas prices and the announcement of a new rationing system, is considered one of the "bloodiest" protests in recent history.[75, 76] When the IRGC accidentally shot down a Ukrainian International Airlines Flight over Tehran after the US killed General Soleimani in January 2020, demonstrators gathered once again, shouting "death to the liars" and "clerics get lost" on university campuses; their frustration was sparked by the government's incompetence and denial of responsibility.[77, 78]

"There is an increasing sense of radicalisation among protesters, while the state is prepared to resort to extreme violence to maintain control," reads a study on the 2019-2020 demonstrations.[79] The significant and growing disconnect between the Iranian regime and the people is evident—not only from the increasingly violent protests, but also from day-to-day interactions: the students mocking the mullah,

---

73 "Iran Poll Shows Only 15 Percent In Tehran Satisfied With Government," Radio Farda, December 22, 2019.

74 "Fact Sheet: Protests in Iran (1979-2019)," United States Institute of Peace: The Iran Primer, last updated January 21, 2020.

75 Ibid.

76 Afshin Shahi and Ehsan Abdoh-Tabrizi, "Iran's 2019-2020 Demonstrations: The Changing Dynamics of Political Protests in Iran," *Asian Affairs* 51, no. 1 (January 2, 2020): 1-41.

77 United States Institute of Peace, "Fact Sheet."

78 Shahi and Abdoh-Tabrizi, "Demonstrations", 1-41.

79 Ibid.

people airing their grievances or indicating hopes of immigration in conversations, and so on.

Even travelers can notice this sentiment: "I feel like Iran is a very polarized country. All this is simmering underneath the surface, and anything could create a lot of turmoil," said Alfred. "I think a lot of [Iranians] are very fed-up. I think everyone is fed-up in their own way. Some are fed up because they believe Iran is going towards a more liberal, reformist path, while others think Iran is still conservative, old-fashioned, and authoritarian." Stark ideological differences exist between the government and the people, between urban and rural, between young and old. He added, "People are so used to the government lying, and the government fabricating history that they just don't trust any of it anymore. I sort of noticed that with a lot of things: the government would say something, and [the people] would automatically do the opposite or believe the opposite."

Yet despite the internal turmoil, regime change is unlikely to happen any time soon. According to a November 2019 brief by the Center for Strategic and International Studies (CSIS), "revolutions—which lead to regime change—have been rare in Iran and other countries" in spite of frequent protests. Among the conditions required for revolution—including centralized and organized collective action, poor or co-optable security forces, a weak economy, and factious elites—many remain absent within Iran. In addition, the government maintains and uses its powerful coercive abilities (through its arrest of protestors, for instance) to protect the regime.[80]

---

80 Seth G. Jones, "Iran's Protests and the Threat to Domestic Stability," Center For Strategic & International Studies (CSIS), November 8, 2019.

Mori, who lives in Tehran, agrees that regime change is unlikely. "This idea of the US government that if they make life difficult for the normal people, they're going to demonstrate against the government, that's absolutely wrong," he said. "That's something that works opposite. People, when they are facing these difficulties, they don't have the motivation to go out and do something. They are just doing their best to meet their daily needs."

Nevertheless, the reality of regime change being unlikely in Iran does not deter foreign politicians from considering it as an option. Foreign voices continue to call for regime change in Iran and advocate for aggressive strategies to do so. As recently as January 2020, a former Pentagon official during the Bush administration, Michael Makovsky, co-wrote an opinion piece in the *Washington Post* titled "The right strategy for Iran isn't regime change. It's regime collapse" arguing for harsher Iran policies to "roll back" Iran's influence in the region.[81] Likewise, Secretary of State Mike Pompeo and National Security Advisor John Bolton, architects of America's Iran policy under Trump, were both loud advocates for regime change prior to entering office.[82] Makovsky's article also argued, "To truly loosen the regime's grip on power and on the region, the United States must explicitly make regime collapse its policy. We don't mean 'regime change' through a US ground invasion, such as Iraq in 2003, but the imposition of consistent, comprehensive pressure, beyond economic

81   Michael Makovsky and Jonathan Ruhe, "The Right Strategy for Iran Isn't Regime Change. It's Regime Collapse.," *The Washington Post*, January 8, 2020.

82   Shahir Shahidsaless, "Why Europe Is Turning against US Policy on Syria and Iran," *Middle East Eye*, last updated November 6, 2018.

sanctions, to exacerbate Iran's internal tensions so that the regime is ultimately undone from within."[83]

Regardless of regime change or the intentions of the US, the repercussions from Iran's instability within the wider region could be dramatic. According to Shahir Shahidsaless, an Iranian-Canadian political analyst, there is no realistic alternative to Iran's current system. If Iran were to be a failed state, the country "could also become home for organised crime, and a major route for drug trafficking between Afghanistan and the West through Turkey. [...] Chaos and civil war could spill over into neighbouring countries and destabilise Turkey and Iraq."[84]

Unlike a military invasion, Americans' lives might not be put on the line by an economic sanctions approach against Iran. Media coverage might not be as shocking or horrific as in the case of a physical war. But the harm from economic sanctions inflicted on the civilian population of Iran—from affording a nutritious diet to having adequate medicine—remains immense and under-acknowledged by international media.

---

83 Makovsky and Ruhe, "Regime Collapse."
84 Shahidsaless, "Why Europe."

CHAPTER 2

WHAT ARE SANCTIONS?

———

Sanctions

"This is a policy instrument of choice... It feels really muscular. We do not have an institutional culture of evaluating economic costs to ourselves, which makes people believe, I think mistakenly, that it is costless."

—ELIZABETH ROSENBERG, FORMER TREASURY DEPARTMENT OFFICIAL[85]

The United States, with the dollar as the predominant currency in international trade, wields significant power over the global economy. Almost two-thirds of the world's central bank reserves are dollars, and the vast majority of international transactions are dollar-denominated.[86] "Even

---

85 Kathy Gilsinan, "A Boom Time for U.S. Sanctions," *The Atlantic*, May 3, 2019.

86 The Economist, "America Must Use Sanctions Cautiously," May 17, 2018.

a company that has basically no trade in the United States, their banks do," says Jarrett Blanc, a senior fellow at the Carnegie Endowment for International Peace, "And so they basically can't be banked if they are trading with a country that has been targeted with these very powerful US sanctions."[87]

Because of the importance of trade and US dollars in modern society, America is granted a large amount of control over the behavior of companies and other countries—and it is not afraid to use this power. As of May 2019, the US has over 7,967 sanctions on more than two dozen countries. Sanctions may often be the choice tool for many of America's foreign policy objectives because they are less expensive and violent than military intervention, but more forceful than just "talking." In recent years, the largest state target of US sanctions is by far Iran—with 700 sanctions levied on the country on one single day in November 2018.[88] To understand US-Iran relations and Iran's current situation under sanctions, this chapter will first provide an overview of sanctions and its usage before providing relevant context on the history of US sanctions in Iran.

Overview

Economic sanctions are measures where a country publicly imposes trade or financial restrictions on a target country to advance political objectives on issues such as nuclear proliferation, terrorism, drug trafficking, human rights violations, or

---

87 Gilsinan, "A Boom Time."
88 Ibid.

democracy promotion.[89, 90] Countries may choose sanctions as the foreign policy tool of choice for a variety of reasons, which can be categorized as "compliance, subversion, deterrence, domestic symbolism, and international symbolism."[91] Though it may be commonly advocated as a non-military foreign policy response, sanctions are nevertheless invasive— having the potential to affect the political, economic, and social conditions of a country.[92]

When are sanctions used? An initiating country may apply sanctions to force the compliance of a target, or to change its behavior in accordance with the former's preferences. Sanctions may also be used as an attempt to damage the economy of a target country where the initiator desires a regime change—under the assumption that economic deterioration would lead to increased political instability. If a country is known to support rebel groups or terrorist organizations, other countries may use sanctions as a means of deterrence or to prevent such actions from happening in the future. A country facing domestic criticism may use sanctions to demonstrate strong, decisive action against other nations to increase domestic support. Or, it could be a means of signaling one country's disapproval of another's behavior to the international community.[93] Sanctions could be imposed on specific individuals, assets, financial

---

89 Dursun Peksen, "When Do Imposed Economic Sanctions Work? A Critical Review of the Sanctions Effectiveness Literature," *Defence and Peace Economics* 30, no. 6 (September 19, 2019): 635-47.

90 James M. Lindsay, "Trade Sanctions as Policy Instruments: A Re-Examination," *International Studies Quarterly* 30, no. 2 (June 1, 1986): 153-73.

91 Ibid.

92 John Forrer, "Economic Sanctions: Sharpening a Vital Foreign Policy Tool," (The Atlantic Council, June 2017).

93 Lindsay, "Trade Sanctions."

institutions, or companies. They can also come in the form of asset freezes, trade embargoes, or travel restrictions.

Who can levy sanctions? Sanctions can be unilaterally or multilaterally enforced: by one nation or by a group of nations—often through the support of international organizations like the UN Security Council. Multilateral sanctions supported by international organizations have been shown to be more effective than either unilateral sanctions or those imposed by a few countries in an ad hoc coalition, as the targeted country has fewer available alternatives and the likelihood of "sanctions-busting" (finding loopholes to evade sanctions restrictions) is decreased with increased sanctions support.[94]

Sanctions directly levied on a target are considered primary sanctions. But in recent decades, secondary sanctions against third-parties that have relations with the target have increasingly been used (particularly by the US) as additional policy measures to prevent sanctions-busting.[95] An entity could serve as a mediator when direct trade is restricted between the sanctions-initiator and the target. In this case, the initiator could impose sanctions on the third-party to deter its further interactions with the target. This third-party facing secondary sanctions could lose access to certain financial services or be banned from conducting business with the initiating country. However, this kind of sanction can be expensive—both economically in terms of trades foregone, but also politically—in terms of distracting from the behaviors of the target, and possibly increasing anti-initiator sentiment or trade disputes with third parties.[96]

---

94 Peksen, "Imposed Economic Sanctions."
95 Ibid.
96 Richard N. Haass, "Economic Sanctions: Too Much of a Bad Thing," Brookings (blog), June 1, 1998.

Until the end of the twentieth century, comprehensive ("conventional") sanctions were typically the type of sanctions used, consisting of broad measures levied against the entire country.[97] Comprehensive sanction policies may include boycotts and embargoes, which refer to a refusal to purchase goods produced by the targeted country and a ban on the supply of goods to the sanctioned buyer, respectively. There have also been cases of a full embargo, where "all economic and trade relations" are cut off in an attempt to isolate the targeted country—such as Cuba in the 1960s.[98]

However, comprehensive sanctions have been known to have "indiscriminate impact," both in the targeted country and on "third countries" that may have been economically dependent on the sanctioned nation.[99] Some of the "well-documented" externalities of conventional sanctions include adverse effects on political freedoms, press freedom, public health and other humanitarian conditions, income inequality, the well-being of disadvantaged segments of society, and ethnic minorities.[100] When Iraq was sanctioned in the 1990s, prominent political groups such as the Sunni minority, the Baath Party, as well as the military and police became more dependent on Saddam Hussein's regime because his rule gave these supporters access to resources that became scarce under sanctions.[101] While Hussein's regime became more repressive, a humanitarian crisis grew—in twelve years, over

---

97 Peksen, "Imposed Economic Sanctions."
98 Maarten Smeets, "Can Economic Sanctions Be Effective? (Working Paper)," World Trade Organization, March 15, 2018, 19.
99 "Smart Sanctions—Targeted Sanctions," State Secretariat for Economic Affairs (SECO), March 24, 2017.
100 Peksen, "Imposed Economic Sanctions."
101 Dursun Peksen, "Better or Worse? The Effect of Economic Sanctions on Human Rights," *Journal of Peace Research* 46, no. 1 (2009): 59-77.

500,000 children died as US and British sanctions denied Iraqi citizens access to food and safe drinking water.[102, 103] According to another estimate, more than 1.5 million Iraqis died as a consequence of scarce food and medicine supplies.[104]

As a result of the "severe negative humanitarian consequences" caused by conventional sanctions, there has been a move in recent decades towards what are known as targeted, or "smart" sanctions. Rather than imposing restrictions on the entire country, smart sanction policies typically consist of trade restrictions on certain goods such as oil or weapons, or financial and travel restrictions on particular individuals, companies, or organizations.[105] In addition, smart sanctions are supposed to provide humanitarian exemptions to food and medical supplies to "cushion" the impact on vulnerable populations.[106]

Yet, as of 2019, there has been "no strong evidence that targeted sanctions are more successful than conventional sanctions."[107] If anything, targeted sanctions have "fail[ed] to achieve their intended objectives more often" than comprehensive sanctions. Similar to the effects of conventional sanctions, targeted sanctions are shown to have "substantially significant negative effects" including increasing poor governance, and corruption, while deteriorating humanitarian

---

102 "Criticism of the Sanctions," Global Policy Forum, accessed November 9, 2020.

103 Per Oskar Klevnas. "Sanctions and the 'Moral Case' for War." Global Policy Forum, March 4, 2003.

104 A. K. Gupta, "Iraq: 'Smart Sanctions' Still Kill," Global Policy Forum, July 2002.

105 SECO, "Smart Sanctions."

106 Arne Tostensen and Beate Bull, "Are Smart Sanctions Feasible?," World Politics 54, no. 3 (April 2002): 373-403.

107 Peksen, "Imposed Economic Sanctions," 5.

conditions and decreasing human development in the targeted country.[108] Moreover, political repression has been shown to increase in spite of targeted and conventional sanctions imposed to promote human rights.[109]

The targeted country is more likely to change its policies when its economy suffers "major damage" from sanctions. However, this works so long as the damage is inflicted on the right groups of people—so that the "balance of power" is tilted in favor of the opposition and damages the leader's legitimacy and coercive capacity. When this is not the case, non-democratic states with high coercive capacity may increase repression while allocating existing resources to the political elites, to the detriment of sanctions objectives and everyday citizens.[110] Shrinkage of the private sector as a consequence of sanctions often contributes to increased government centralization and state capacity, thereby bolstering authoritarian governments.[111, 112] For instance, even while under sanctions, Saddam Hussein was able to illegally export billions of dollars' worth of oil. Whereas legal exports were controlled by the UN and paid for Iraqi citizens' humanitarian needs, the money from the illicit oil trade went directly to Saddam's regime—which he then used to pay political supporters and hold onto power.[113]

---

108 Ibid, 6.
109 Ibid.
110 Ibid, 5.
111 Hassan Hakimian, "Seven Key Misconceptions about Economic Sanctions," World Economic Forum, May 9, 2019.
112 Haass, "Economic Sanctions."
113 Abel Escribà-Folch and Joseph Wright, "Dealing with Tyranny: International Sanctions and the Survival of Authoritarian Rulers," International Studies Quarterly 54, no. 2 (2010): 335-59.

Since the late twentieth century, sanctions have been used with increasing frequency, oftentimes considered as an alternative to more violent forms of coercion. However, using sanctions as a "gentler and more humane alternative to war" undermines the effectiveness of diplomacy and negotiation. In practice, sanctions have often preceded harsher responses, "pav[ing] the way" to war rather than avoiding it.[114] The invasion of Iraq in 2003 occurred after over a decade of sanctions on the country.[115]

When the US imposed an oil embargo on Japan and seized its assets in 1940-41, Japanese leaders "saw little distinction between economic sanctions and warfare and realized that sanctions would make their country weaker over time—something that encouraged them to strike sooner rather than later."[116] Japan struck Pearl Harbor that year in December. Even if direct military conflict is highly unlikely in the contemporary context, a targeted country—fearing its survival is at stake—may "inflict pain" on the initiating country in an attempt to ease sanctions through proxy warfare, engaging in terrorism, or other forms of indirect conflict.[117]

In general, sanctions are more likely to achieve their policy objectives when these goals are "less ambitious," or when coupled with other policy measures. Whereas using economic sanctions to negotiate the release of a political prisoner is likely to work, implementing trade restrictions

114 Hakimian, "Seven Key Misconceptions."
115 Ibid.
116 Paul J. Saunders, "When Sanctions Lead to War," *The New York Times*, August 21, 2014, sec. Opinion.
117 Gilles Van Nederveen, "Do Sanctions Lead to War?," *Foreign Policy Journal*, January 7, 2012.

as a means to engender regime change is not only unlikely to succeed, but risks further deterioration of political freedoms in the target country.[118] North Korea, Cuba, and Myanmar are some examples of countries whose regimes have withstood decades of economic isolation.[119] North Korea, Cuba, and Zimbabwe are also three of four countries that have developed nuclear capabilities in the past fifty years despite sanctions.[120] Over time, many regimes adapt to economic isolation and international coordination diminishes, causing "sanctions fatigue" and eroding their impact.

Nevertheless, sanctions were "one factor" that contributed to Serbia's acceptance of the Dayton Accords that ended the war in Bosnia, and in Libya the use of sanctions to "focus on engaged bargaining" led Qaddafi to renounce its nuclear program, among other things.[121] Other examples of "less ambitious" sanctions objectives that have "tend[ed] to work better" include restricting a country's access to resources and using the tool for domestic or international symbolism. However, even when the short-term policy objectives that led to sanctions use are achieved, the negative effects of sanctions on a country are likely to persist in the long-term.[122]

Due to the varying degrees of effectiveness, the debate about the use of sanctions remains contentious. By studying the impacts of sanctions in the past, research has established guidelines for implementing a sanctions regime as effectively as possible:

---

118 Peksen, "Imposed Economic Sanctions."
119 Hakimian, "Seven Key Misconceptions."
120 Hassan Hakimian, How Sanctions Affect Iran's Economy, interview by Toni Johnson, May 22, 2012.
121 Haass, "Economic Sanctions."
122 Peksen, "Imposed Economic Sanctions."

"Economic sanctions are more effective in achieving their policy objectives if they are multilateral sanctions led by international institutions; if they exact significant economic costs on the target economy; if they are directed at allies rather than rivals; if they are imposed with moderate policy goals rather than ambitious ones such as regime change."[123]

Yet achieving the ideal implementation of sanctions can be difficult: it requires a high degree of information about the targeted country and must be dynamic—adjusting to the fluctuations of the global economy.[124] In practice, sanctions can remain on a country for a very long period of time—like those experienced in Iran or Iraq, with no limits to the amount of damage, no exit strategy, and sometimes no clear objective. As a foreign policy tool, sanctions might not be inherently bad. However, when used inappropriately, they could lead to a variety of unintended consequences and inflict disproportionate and long-term harm on the civilian population.

Human Rights Effect of Sanctions

There is a wealth of existing literature on the effectiveness of the various sanctions on Iran. This book will refrain from any extensive discussion of the political aspects of economic sanctions or whether they have achieved the initiating country's political objectives. Rather, it aims to highlight the humanitarian consequences of comprehensive sanctions

---

123 Ibid.
124 Forrer, "Sharpening a Vital Foreign Policy Tool."

policies, particularly in the past decade. Sanctions regimes that are generally deemed "successful" may be equally problematic as those that are "unsuccessful." Although both scenarios may have similarly damaging human rights effects on the civilian population, the former also provides a dangerous precedent to policymakers, whereby its positive connotation likely diminishes the humanitarian suffering endured for years by ordinary citizens.

As articulated by Amnesty International, "sanctions imposed by the USA continued to negatively impact Iran's economy, with detrimental consequences for the enjoyment of economic, social and cultural rights."[125] These rights include the right to work, the right to an adequate standard of living (i.e. food, clothing, and housing), the right to both physical and mental health, the right to social security, the right to a healthy environment, and the right to education.[126] Many of these rights require the support of the government and other institutions to provide necessary systems and infrastructure. The economic impact of sanctions has damaging effects on any government's ability to ensure these rights.

The achievement of economic, social, and cultural rights, and civil and political rights are interconnected.[127] As written by Héctor Gros Espiell, a member of the Inter-American Court of Human Rights, in 1986, "Only the full recognition of all of these rights can guarantee the real existence of any one of them, since without the effective enjoyment of

---

125 "Iran 2019," Amnesty International, accessed October 21, 2020.
126 "What Are Economic, Social and Cultural Rights?," Center for Economic and Social Rights (CESR), December 3, 2008.
127 "Key Concepts on ESCRs—Are Economic, Social and Cultural Rights Fundamentally Different from Civil and Political Rights?," United Nations Human Rights Office of the High Commissioner (OHCHR), accessed October 21, 2020.

economic, social and cultural rights, civil and political rights are reduced to merely formal categories. Conversely, without the reality of civil and political rights, without effective liberty understood in its broadest sense, economic, social and cultural rights in turn lack any real significance."[128]

In practice, the interdependence of these categories of rights is omnipresent. For example, judges, the military, and the police are necessary to ensure both civil and political rights. However, the process of training these people requires resources—not only in terms of education, but also in the provision of basic necessities such as food, clothing, housing, and healthcare. Or, the protection of someone's right to shelter (an economic and social right) requires a society that respects civil and political rights and the rule of law. Political actors have the ability to prevent famine and starvation, and education allows people to participate politically in society.[129]

In the case of Iran, there have been "unprecedented" uprisings in recent years. Those who are dissatisfied with their economic and social conditions have taken to the streets in increasing frequency and scale, only to be arrested for threatening the stability of the regime. Described as the "movement of the hungry," most of the arrested protesters were "unemployed or low-income."[130]

If the US is to be an advocate for human rights on an international level and especially in Iran—by imposing travel bans and sanctions on officials who commit human rights

---

128 Flavia Piovesan, "Social, Economic and Cultural Rights and Civil and Political Rights," *Sur—International Journal on Human Rights*, August 10, 2017.

129 Elif Gözler Çamur, "Civil and Political Rights vs. Social and Economic Rights: A Brief Overview," *Journal of Bitlis Eren University Institute of Social Sciences* 6, no. 1 (2017): 205-14.

130 Shahidsaless, "Retaliation Is More than a Matter of Saving Face."

violations—then a broader framework that, at the minimum, focuses on preserving human rights is requisite in its foreign policy. Economic, social, and cultural rights are equally important as civil and political rights. It is therefore counterproductive to support one set of rights in US foreign policy while sacrificing another in other policies.

A Brief History of Sanctions in Iran

The first round of sanctions imposed on Iran was during the 1979 hostage crisis at the apex of the Islamic Revolution. As mentioned earlier, a group of radical students took over the US embassy on the 4th of November, demanding the return of the "criminal, deposed Shah," who was in the US seeking cancer treatment.[131] The Iran Hostage Crisis lasted 444 days, and fifty-two Americans were taken hostage. Negotiation attempts and rescue missions failed, until the Algiers Accord was signed between the US and Iran in January 1981.

Many fascinating books have been written about Iran and its momentous Islamic Revolution, notably Michael Axworthy's *Revolutionary Iran: A History of the Islamic Republic*. For the purposes of this book, it will suffice to say that the hostage crisis was an unprecedented event in the context of international relations, and the images of Americans held captive at the embassy—handcuffed and blindfolded—made a "deep impression" in the US and changed the nature of US-Iran relations.[132]

---

131 Axworthy, *Revolutionary Iran*, 168.
132 Ibid.

The crisis was the first time that America imposed sanctions against Iran, in an effort to secure the release of the hostages. "Nearly all Iranian assets" held in the US were blocked, "virtually all US trade with Iran" was banned, and by April 1980, President Carter had severed diplomatic relations with the country. From then until the end of the twentieth century, Iran posed a threat to US interests in the Middle East. Most US sanctions during this period have therefore had the objective of preventing the spread of Iran's influence—through its support for "acts of terrorism" or other means of acquiring "strategic power" in the region.[133]

In addition to the hostage crisis, another sequence of events that unfolded during the revolution eventually led to the Iran-Iraq War. Throughout 1979, the old monarchy was toppled, a national referendum declared the new country an Islamic republic, and by December, Ayatollah Ruhollah Khomeini was named "Iran's political and religious leader for life."[134] Among other pronouncements, Khomeini used Iran's revolution as a religious platform, calling for Shia populations across the Middle East to "rise up."[135]

Meanwhile, Saddam Hussein had been elected president in July 1979 in neighboring Iraq and was head of a "Sunni-dominated, secular government" to rule a majority-Shia population.[136] Having spent a period of his exile in Iraq prior to Iran's revolution, Khomeini's words "resonated" with Iraqi

---

133 Kenneth Katzman, "Iran Sanctions" (Congressional Research Service), last updated July 23, 2020.

134 "Ruhollah Khomeini," Encyclopedia Britannica, accessed October 21, 2020.

135 Ariane Tabatabai and Annie Tracy Samuel, "Understanding the Iran Nuclear Deal through the Lens of the Iran-Iraq War," *Lawfare*, July 16, 2017.

136 Ibid.

Shias, prompting certain Iraqi clergy members to "try to take power in their own right."[137] Iran in the midst of its revolution was fragile, and the combination of oil incentives and Shia threat made Iran an attractive target for Iraq. In September 1980, Saddam Hussein launched an Iraqi invasion of Iran. Although the attack was expected to be "swift and easy," it devolved into an eight-year war that incurred over half a million total deaths—costing hundreds of thousands of lives on both sides.[138, 139]

Throughout the war, the US, Soviet Union, Europe, and Arab countries provided weapons, technology, intelligence, and other forms of assistance to Iraq. For weeks after Iraq's invasion, neither the US nor other permanent UN Security Council members called for a meeting about the issue or demanded Iraqi withdrawal. The US provided intelligence that not only helped foil Iran's counterattacks but also "directly facilitated Iraq's use of chemical weapons."[140, 141] It was "the only war in modern times" where chemical weapons were used on a "massive scale" along with ballistic missiles. Eventually, to protect oil tankers passing through the Strait of Hormuz, the US directly intervened in the war in 1988. An "undeclared naval war" ensued, wherein a US navy cruiser directly shot down an Iranian civilian airliner, killing all 290 passengers.[142, 143]

Relative to the support that Iraq had received, Iran was fighting the devastating war in international isolation, with

137 Axworthy, *Revolutionary Iran*, 97.
138 Tabatabai and Samuel, "Understanding the Iran Nuclear Deal."
139 Bruce Riedel, "How the Iran-Iraq War Shaped the Trajectories of Figures like Qassem Soleimani," Brookings (blog), January 9, 2020.
140 Ibid.
141 "How Saddam Happened" (2002).
142 Riedel, "Qassem Soleimani."
143 Tabatabai and Samuel, "Understanding the Iran Nuclear Deal."

Syria as "one of [its] few dependable allies." Although Iran was desperate for weapons, it was "short of money and short of friends" who were willing to supply equipment.[144] As a result, Iran became increasingly aware that, for the sake of the country's survival, it needed to become "self-reliant in matters of defense."[145]

Among other experiences following the hostage crisis that emphasized Iran's global isolation, the Iran-Iraq war drove home the need for Iran to resume and upgrade its defense capabilities—despite Khomeini's initial opposition to nuclear technology. Iran's nuclear program had begun under the Shah in the 1950s through the US Atoms for Peace initiative. Due to both a lack of political support and talent (nuclear scientists fled the country in the midst of the revolution), Iran's nuclear program in 1979 was at a state of "near disintegration." However, by the end of the Iran-Iraq war, Iran was beginning partnerships with Pakistan, and later China and Russia, to help develop its nuclear program.[146]

From the early-2000s onwards, sanctions against Iran have primarily been levied against the country's continued development of nuclear weapons technology.[147] Many talks have been attempted and failed throughout the years, often because Iran is seeking more immediate sanctions relief than negotiating countries are willing to grant in exchange for the suspension of its nuclear program.[148] Due to Iran's failure to comply with international agreements, sanctions in the early 2000s imposed travel bans, asset freezes, and other

---

144 Axworthy, *Revolutionary Iran*, 232.
145 Tabatabai and Samuel, "Understanding the Iran Nuclear Deal."
146 "Iran: Nuclear," Nuclear Threat Initiative (NTI), last updated June 2020.
147 Katzman, "Iran Sanctions."
148 NTI, "Iran: Nuclear."

financial restrictions on individuals affiliated with Iran's nuclear program.[149, 150] However, these were predominantly enforced unilaterally by the US, and were "not very strong."[151]

In 2010 the US "stepped up its sanctions," and through diplomatic efforts, began forming a coalition not only with Europe but also "loosely" with Russia and China to establish a relatively united front against Iran's nuclear program.[152] The UN Security Council Resolution 1929 of that year reiterated demands for Iran to halt its development of nuclear weapons and incorporated a sixth round of sanctions, which included an arms embargo and a prohibition of the transfer of ballistic missile technology to the country.[153]

From then on until 2013, the P5+1 consisting of Germany and the five permanent members of the security council (United States, France, UK, China, and Russia) engaged in a "dual-track" approach towards Iran's nuclear program— engaging in sanctions and negotiations, in order to establish a "negotiated settlement" between the parties involved.[154] Of note is the 2011 Menendez-Kirk amendment, which included US sanctions against Iran's Central Bank and secondary sanctions on foreign financial institutions that continued to process oil and petroleum-related transactions from Iran if they failed to significantly reduce their purchases.[155] Attempts at talks con-

---

149 Ibid.

150 Kelsey Davenport, "UN Security Council Resolutions on Iran," Arms Control Association (ACA), last reviewed August 2017.

151 Gary Clyde Hufbauer, Sanctions on Iran: Why They Worked and Why a "Snapback" May Not Work, interview by Steve Weisman, March 2, 2016.

152 Ibid.

153 Davenport, "Resolutions on Iran."

154 Ibid.

155 "Menendez, Kirk Amendment for Stronger Sanctions Against Iran Passes Unanimously in the Senate," Bob Menendez for Senate, December 1, 2011.

tinued (although with no real progress) while the intensity of sanctions increased to "drag Iran to the negotiating table."[156]

When a Security Council resolution for another round of sanctions was blocked by China and Russia—perhaps due to economic interests—the US and Europe each imposed "unprecedented" unilateral sanctions on Iran. In 2013, President Obama authorized an executive order to impose secondary sanctions on foreign financial institutions that "[conducted] 'significant transactions' using the Iranian rial... or [maintained] rial accounts outside Iran."[157] During this period of relative international coordination, sanctions had a sharp and significant impact on Iran's economy. It became "very cumbersome for Iran either to buy or sell much of anything" and interrupted Iran's oil exports—the country's primary source of foreign currency—essentially restricting Iran's access to the global financial system.[158]

When centrist Hassan Rouhani was elected to become the president of Iran in June 2013, there was a "shift" in Iran's position regarding negotiations.[159, 160] As Iran's chief nuclear negotiator from 2003 to 2005, Rouhani expressed his desire as president to resume talks as a means of "elevating Iran's position based on national interest" and prioritizing the "lifting of the oppressive sanctions". By November 24th, 2013, a temporary Joint Plan of Action (JPOA) had been reached as a preliminary step towards a more comprehensive agreement.[161] The P5+1 provided Iran with "limited" sanctions easing.

---

156 Hufbauer, interview.
157 NTI, "Iran: Nuclear."
158 Hufbauer, interview.
159 NTI, "Iran: Nuclear."
160 Hakimian, "Seven Key Misconceptions."
161 NTI, "Iran: Nuclear."

Amongst other provisions, certain US-Iran trade restrictions were suspended, and Iran was granted $65 million per month "to make tuition payments for Iranian students abroad."[162] In return, Iran worked with the International Atomic Energy Agency (IAEA) to freeze its nuclear program and diminish its "most proliferation-sensitive elements."[163]

Negotiation for a more comprehensive deal was an extensive process. Teams on both sides "remain[ed] in the [...] hotel in Vienna, Austria" beyond the intended negotiation deadline "until an agreement could be reached."[164] To reach an agreement, President Obama reassured Iran that regime change was "off the table" and conceded for Iran to enrich uranium domestically.[165] The combination of intense diplomatic efforts and sanctions was applied for the singular objective of "effectively cut[ting] off all Iran's pathways to enough fissile material for a nuclear weapon."[166]

Finally, on July 14th, 2015, the Iran Deal, formally known as the Joint Comprehensive Plan of Action (JCPOA), was achieved. It was signed by Britain, China, the EU, Iran, France, Germany, Russia, and the United States.[167] Iran's nuclear program would be capped by a "break-out time"—so that it would eventually require at least a year to produce

162 Katzman, "Iran Sanctions."

163 Kelsey Davenport, "Implementation of the Joint Plan of Action At A Glance," Arms Control Association (ACA), last reviewed August 2017.

164 NTI, "Iran: Nuclear."

165 Ali Vaez, "Missing the Point on Iran's Nuclear Breakout Time," The International Crisis Group, March 2, 2015.

166 "The Historic Deal That Will Prevent Iran from Acquiring a Nuclear Weapon," The White House—President Barack Obama, accessed October 21, 2020.

167 Colum Lynch, "Despite U.S. Sanctions, Iran Expands Its Nuclear Stockpile," Foreign Policy, May 8, 2020.

an Iranian nuclear weapon.[168] If Iran remained compliant in rolling back its nuclear program, sanctions relief from the United States, Europe, and the United Nations would be lifted in various phases.

By Implementation Day on January 16th, 2016, the IAEA had given Iran the green light, acknowledging its compliance with the conditions of the JCPOA that involved "key steps" towards limiting its nuclear program. UN and EU sanctions related to Iran's nuclear program were lifted, while arms embargoes and restrictions on ballistic missiles remained. The US suspended its secondary sanctions, but it continued to prohibit most forms of direct US-Iran trade and enforce sanctions against Iran's "human rights, terrorism and missile activities."[169]

Although Iran continued to comply with the terms under the JCPOA, US policy toward Iran drastically changed when Trump became president.[170] Forgoing Obama's attempts to re-open channels of communication with Iran, the Trump Administration has led a "maximum pressure" campaign that has re-imposed pre-JCPOA sanctions in an attempt to renegotiate a deal. Within 180 days of the US withdrawal from the JCPOA in May 2018, foreign businesses had to sever contracts and end business relationships with Iran.[171] Shortly afterward, Iran lost access to the global market—foreign currency, global banking systems, and oil exports were once again restricted.[172]

The US claims the objective of its new round of sanctions

---

168 NTI, "Iran: Nuclear."
169 Davenport, "Joint Plan of Action."
170 NTI, "Iran: Nuclear."
171 Katzman, "Iran Sanctions."
172 Katrina Manson, "What the US Withdrawal from the Iran Nuclear Deal Means," *The Financial Times*, May 9, 2018.

is to deny Iran funding for its military and force Iran back to the negotiating table to create a new deal that would limit its missile program and curb its "malign activities" in the region.[173, 174] Though there are many interpretations of why the US withdrew from the JCPOA, the Trump Administration has stated its reasons to be the incompleteness of the deal's terms and Iran's violation of the "spirit" of the agreement. The US has cited the sunset clause (i.e. the impermanence of the deal) as well as its exclusion of ballistic missile testing to be primary reasons for leaving the JCPOA. A senior Administration official stated, "If the President can get that agreement that meets his objectives and that never expires... he would be open to remaining in such a modified deal."[175]

Whereas the JCPOA would make nuclear weapons unattainable to Iran for "at least fifteen years," this Administration sought an agreement that would permanently deny Iran any path to creating a nuclear weapon.[176, 177] Trump also referred to conflicts between American and Iranian interests in the Middle East as a reason for leaving the deal: "The Iranian regime supports terrorism and exports violence, bloodshed and chaos across the Middle East. That is why we must put an end to Iran's continued aggression and nuclear ambitions. They have not lived up to the spirit of their agreement."[178]

---

173 "Iran Sanctions/Europe in on-Record Briefing by Special Representative for Iran Brian Hook (November 2)," U.S. Embassy in Georgia, November 2, 2018.

174 Katzman, "Iran Sanctions."

175 "Background Press Call on Iran Sanctions," The White House, January 12, 2018.

176 Ibid.

177 "Understanding the Iran Deal: What, Why and the next Steps," *Al Jazeera*, May 8, 2019.

178 Ibid.

Yet according to the Director of the Stockholm International Peace Research Institute, Dan Smith, Trump's reversal of a signature Obama-era foreign policy achievement was "a political measure aimed against Iran" rather than "an evidence-based technical objection to the agreement or its implementation."[179] However, the United States' increasingly harsh sanctions and Iran's unmet conditions—such as sanctions relief—have led to a further breakdown of US-Iran relations and the latter's refusal to restart negotiations.[180]

Globally, the US exit from the JCPOA has been met with disapproval: "The US action undermines the global effort for nuclear non-proliferation by sabotaging an important and effective anti-proliferation agreement," writes Smith. The act not only "challeng[ed] the authority of the UN Security Council," but also diminished global trust in the IAEA.[181] Countries like France, Germany, the UK, and Russia reiterated their support for the deal, while the UN Secretary-General, Antonio Guterres, expressed his "concern."[182] Former Secretary of State John Carry said, "Instead of building on unprecedented nonproliferation verification measures, this decision risks throwing them away and dragging the world back to the brink we faced a few years ago."[183]

European nations attempted to salvage the deal by creating the Instrument in Support of Trade Exchanges (INSTEX) in September 2018 in efforts to continue trade with Iran. This

179 Dan Smith, "The US Withdrawal from the Iran Deal: One Year On," Stockholm International Peace Research Institute (SIPRI), May 7, 2019.
180 Katzman, "Iran Sanctions."
181 Smith, "The US Withdrawal."
182 NTI, "Iran: Nuclear."
183 Mark Landler, "Trump Abandons Iran Nuclear Deal He Long Scorned (Published 2018)," *The New York Times*, May 8, 2018, sec. World.

entity is intended to act as a clearinghouse for transactions between Iran and Europe without requiring US dollars. However, after receiving heavy criticism from the US, the instrument originally designed to bypass US sanctions has become limited to trading only non-sanctionable items such as humanitarian goods. Trade volume through INSTEX was small initially and is expected to "remain small."[184]

The EU's attempts to salvage the deal, such as a blocking statute that protects European companies from consequences of certain secondary sanctions, also seem unlikely to have a significant impact—companies are likely to remain risk-averse, especially when faced with the threat of losing access to the US financial system. Iran has therefore not been able to receive any of the economic relief from exporting oil which had been expected to occur under the original INSTEX plan.[185]

In response to Europe's failure to revive the deal and worsening domestic economic conditions, Iran has continued its phases of reduced compliance with the JCPOA.[186] The deterioration of the JCPOA has put significant pressure on the Iranian President from domestic opposition such as "clerical and security hard-liners"—many of whom raised disagreements when the deal was first signed.[187] Iranians' opinions have also changed: while over 85 percent of people

---

184 Chase Winter, "What Is the EU-Iran Payment Vehicle INSTEX?," DW.COM, accessed October 21, 2020.

185 Burt Braverman and Dsu-Wei Yuen, "EU Companies Face Tough Choice: Violate U.S. Secondary Sanctions on Iran or Amended EU Blocking Regulations," Lexology, accessed October 21, 2020.

186 Hufbauer, Interview.

187 Winter, "EU-Iran Payment."

supported the deal in 2015, by 2019 more than half of those surveyed wanted Iran to "quit" the JCPOA.[188]

US sanctions on Iran have effectively dismantled the deal, as the incentives for Iran to remain have dissolved: "If we cannot sell our oil and we don't enjoy financial transactions, then I don't think keeping the deal will benefit us anymore," said Ali Akbar Salehi, the head of Iran's Atomic Energy Organization.[189] Two years following Trump's withdrawal from the JCPOA, Iran had "cut in half" the time required for it to produce a nuclear weapon.[190]

Though not much progress has been made to prevent Iran from getting closer to creating a nuclear weapon, Trump Administration Officials have cited limitations on Iran's ability to pay to Hezbollah and reductions in the country's capacity to project power in the region as evidence for the sanctions' success.[191] But fundamentally, Iran's regional strategy remains unchanged.[192] In September 2019, three months after the US Special Representative for Iran, Brian Hook, testified to the House Foreign Affairs Committee on Iran's decreased military budget, the country instigated drone and missile attacks on Saudi Arabian oil production facilities.[193] Though spending limitations may reduce the choices available for Iran to effectuate its foreign policy, provocations will continue so long as the country believes itself to be under threat.

---

188 Barbara Slavin, "Majority of Iranians Now Want to Quit Nuclear Deal," Al-Monitor, October 16, 2019.

189 Winter, "EU-Iran Payment."

190 Lynch, "Despite U.S. Sanctions."

191 Katzman, "Iran Sanctions", 50.

192 Tabatabai and Samuel, "Understanding the Iran Nuclear Deal."

193 Stratfor Worldview, "Iran May Up Its Aggression As the U.S. Expands Sanctions," RealClear Defense, November 5, 2019.

So far, Iran's response to the JCPOA has been measured, and there has been "no evidence [that] Tehran is preparing a dash for a nuclear weapon."[194] In fact, to the knowledge of the US intelligence community, Iran has possessed the capacity scientifically and practically to produce nuclear weapons since 2007. Rather than being a skills issue, the acquisition of a nuclear weapon is instead a political calculation dependent upon Iran's "perception of their threat environment."[195] A report by the International Crisis Group wrote, "If leaders in Tehran believe that their survival requires the ultimate deterrent, they would likely be willing to endure even more punishing sanctions to acquire the bomb."[196] If this is true, sanctions that threaten the regime's survival may quicken the pace of Iran's nuclear timeline, instead of slowing it down.

194 Lynch, "Despite U.S. Sanctions."
195 Vaez, "Missing the Point."
196 Ibid.

PART II

———

CHAPTER 3

SANCTIONS' EFFECTS ON THE ECONOMY

———

Jetlagged and in need of a shower, we grabbed a taxi immediately upon landing at Tehran's Imam Khomeini International Airport—a large, flat glass building with high ceilings in a style typical of many airports. As we rode into the city center filled with brown-grey buildings dotted by occasional mosques with colorful tiling, my friend Nicolas noticed that all the cars on the busy street looked the same. "Like white boxes," he thought aloud. That was the first time he noticed how the country was impacted by sanctions: everyone was purchasing the same locally manufactured model of vehicle. Recalling that moment to me later on, Nicolas said: "It's just quite obvious that in terms of manufacturing, that much is done in Iran… Iran doesn't have that many options."

Overview

Although sanctions have been imposed on Iran long before the sanctions under Obama that began in 2011, they were relatively unilateral and had limited effects on the economy. The Iranian government back then was largely able to counteract the increasing costs of sanctions and mitigate problems that stemmed from its own mismanagement by lubricating the economy with oil imports. However, under the Ahmadinejad presidency between 2005-2013, Iran's finances worsened as the country became more dependent on oil; the government increasingly borrowed from banks, and in turn grew more reliant on the Iranian Central Bank.[197, 198] Ahmadinejad also expanded the Iran Revolutionary Guard Corps (IRGC)—the government's "security and coercive apparatus"—control of the economy.[199] The IRGC's hold over the service, manufacturing, and commercial sectors amounted to at least a third of the Iranian economy—which, as will be explained later, has had a detrimental effect on legitimate business development and foreign investment.[200]

Given the condition of the economy in the early 2010s— i.e. increased dependence on oil profits, reliance on the Central Bank, and IRGC control over industries—the coordinated sanctions regime in the early 2010s struck a devastating blow that exacerbated existing economic weaknesses.

197 Razieh Zahedi and Pooya Azadi, "Central Banking in Iran," Stanford University, Stanford Iran 2040 Project, Working Paper No. 5 (June 2018): 38.

198 "A Growing Crisis: The Impact of Sanctions and Regime Policies on Iranians' Economic and Social Rights," International Campaign for Human Rights in Iran (ICHRI), 2013.

199 Ibid.

200 "Six Charts That Show How Hard US Sanctions Have Hit Iran," *BBC News*, December 9, 2019.

Europe and the UN cooperated alongside the US in targeting critical points such as the Central Bank, the IRGC, and oil exports. By 2012, the Iranian economy entered "full-fledged stagflation" and economic activities plunged.[201] The then-US Treasury Secretary Timothy Geithner stated that sanctions had caused Iran's economy to shrink by 20 percent.[202] GDP growth rate fell to a twenty-year low of -7.4 percent, the rial lost half its value, and the inflation rate rose to around 40 percent.[203, 204] The budget deficit increased.[205]

When the JCPOA provided sanctions relief in the 2016-2018 period, Iran's economy became one of the fastest-growing in the world, and inflation fell to record lows.[206] In 2016, the GDP growth rate reached a twenty-five year high of 13.4 percent.[207] There was a "record number" of new jobs created in the year following March 2017, with non-oil sectors accounting for the "overwhelming majority" of growth that the country experienced[208]. The agriculture and services industries, in addition to oil, recovered to activity levels experienced prior to the 2011/12 sanctions regime.[209] Foreign Direct Investment

201 Zahedi and Azadi, "Central Banking."
202 Bozorgmehr Sharafedin, "Iranian Jobs Go as U.S. Sanctions Start to Bite," *Reuters*, November 19, 2018.
203 "GDP Growth (Annual %)—Iran, Islamic Rep. | Data," World Bank, accessed October 21, 2020.
204 Zahedi and Azadi, "Central Banking."
205 Sajjad Faraji Dizaji, "The Effects of Oil Shocks on Government Expenditures and Government Revenues Nexus (with an Application to Iran's Sanctions)," *Economic Modelling* 40, no. C (2014): 299-313.
206 "Iran Economic Monitor: Weathering Economic Challenges" (World Bank Group, Fall 2018).
207 László Csicsmann, "Struggling for a Sustainable Economy: Iran after the JCPOA," MENARA Future Notes no. 19, March 2019.
208 World bank, "Iran Economic Monitor."
209 Ibid.

(FDI) increased by as much as 50 percent in 2017, and Iran's trade with Europe nearly doubled in 2018—with companies like Norway's Saga Energy committing $3 billion to build solar power plants, Germany's Siemens to upgrade the railway system, and France's Renault to build an engineering center and production factory in Iran.[210, 211] Despite the "overwhelmingly positive" effects of sanctions relief, most Iranians did not reap the benefits of economic growth, and inequality remains a longer-term issue within the country.[212] Moreover, economic recovery was hampered by many firms that did not re-enter the Iranian market during this period, doubting that the deal would stay intact.[213]

When sanctions were snapped back on Iran in 2018, the economy experienced a downturn similar to that in the early-2010s. Within four months of the US withdrawal from the JCPOA, the Consumer Price Index (CPI) inflation more than tripled to the highest point since 2013. This increase in the basket of consumer goods was so rapid that the August 2018 rate was the largest recorded jump since inflation data became available in 2002.[214] The rial lost around 70 percent of its value against the dollar, and the exchange rate has since fluctuated.[215] While $1 had cost approximately 42,000 rials for ordinary Iranians prior to the sanctions, within two months the

210 Shora Azarnoush, "Iran's Economy Plummets under Weight of Sanctions," DW.COM, October 23, 2019.

211 Sharafedin, "Iranian Jobs."

212 Csicsmann, "Struggling for a Sustainable Economy."

213 Zachary Laub and Kali Robinson, "What Is the Status of the Iran Nuclear Agreement?," Council on Foreign Relations, last updated January 7, 2020.

214 World Bank, "Iran Economic Monitor".

215 Thomas Erdbrink, "Iran's Economic Crisis Drags Down the Middle Class Almost Overnight (Published 2018)," *The New York Times*, December 26, 2018, sec. World.

equivalent conversion amounted to 160,000 rials. Less than two years after these sanctions came into effect, the equivalent of $1 is about 317,000 rials. Europe's attempts to continue trade with Iran could not sufficiently mitigate the latter's economic decline. According to the October 2020 World Economic Outlook by the International Monetary Fund (IMF), Iran's GDP contracted by 5.4 percent in 2018 and decreased by a further 6.5 percent in 2019.[216, 217] The World Bank also predicted that Iran's economy will shrink by 90 percent within two years by 2020.[218] From the high growth rates of the JCPOA era, Iran between 2017 and 2019 fell amidst the "small number of economies" in the world that was "under severe distress."[219]

In general, both sanctions periods—before and after relief granted by the JCPOA—have had similarly detrimental economic and humanitarian effects on Iran. Banking and import restrictions and sanctions-induced inflationary spirals have affected businesses, unemployment, and Iranians' standard of living. Since 2019, the Central Bank of Iran has stopped issuing any reports on the economy due to the "havoc" caused by the US sanctions.[220] Nevertheless, the World Bank predicted at the end of 2018 that Iran would undergo "similar declines in growth and inflationary pressures" as was experienced under the previous round of sanctions in the early 2010s.[221] Iranian locals affirm that their

---

216 *BBC News,* "Six Charts."

217 "World Economic Outlook: Global Manufacturing Downturn, Rising Trade Barriers," International Monetary Fund (IMF), (Washington, DC, October 2019).

218 "Iran's Economic Update—October 2019," World Bank, October 9, 2019.

219 IMF, "World Economic Outlook," 9.

220 "Iran's Statistical Center Reports 7.6 Percent Decline in GDP," Radio Farda, February 10, 2020.

221 World Bank, "Iran Economic Monitor."

experience of the recent sanctions has been "more or less the same" as the earlier period. "I can lie and say that this time the government is more prepared, but they are not," a local from Isfahan admitted when we spoke on the topic.

While the following section explains how US sanctions have impacted different aspects of Iran's economy, it is important to note that Iran is not the only country affected economically by sanctions. According to the National Iranian American Council (NIAC), from 1995 to 2012, America has given up between $135 billion and $175 billion in export revenue by refusing to do business with Iran.[222]

Sanctions' Effects on Different Aspects of the Economy

What do these numbers about GDP, inflation, and employment mean in reality? This chapter will first examine the effects of sanctions on oil (as a major source of government revenue), inflation, and business, which will provide context for the situation of Iranian locals and how existing problems are aggravated by economic sanctions.

Oil and Government Capacity

Although direct US sanctions against Iranian oil have existed since the late 1980s,[223] the coordinated international pressure against Iran around 2010-2012 for nuclear negotiations

---

222 Ishaan Tharoor, "Sanctions on Iran Cost the U.S. as Much as $175 Billion, Study Says," *The Washington Post*, July 16, 2014.

223 Katzman, "Iran Sanctions."

made it significantly more difficult for Iran to trade its oil globally. Equipment and technology related to natural gas production were banned, secondary sanctions were imposed on banks and companies that conducted business with Iran's oil industry, Iran's central bank—the primary clearinghouse for oil-related transactions—was also sanctioned, and the EU enforced an oil embargo along with the US.[224] More recently in 2019, the White House announced the intention to "bring Iran's oil exports to zero."[225] The US announced its aims to "[deny] the regime its principal source of revenue," while supplementing the loss of Iranian oil in the global market with oil from the US, UAE, and Saudi Arabia.[226] According to Trump, this plan would hold Iran's leaders accountable for "plunder[ing] the nation's resources to enrich themselves and to spread mayhem across the Middle East and far beyond."[227]

Reducing the resources available to Iran's central government may mean a decrease in Iran's ability to provide financial assistance to regional proxy wars, but it also means a decrease in the government's overall capacity to support its citizens—especially as oil accounts for approximately 40 percent of Iran's government revenue.[228] Under the 2012 sanctions, Iran's cash-strapped government lost its ability to pay employees on time—including IRGC soldiers.[229] Its payments to contractors were also delayed, further affecting factories and businesses and their ability to pay their workers.

---

224 "Timeline: Sanctions on Iran," Al Jazeera, October 17, 2012.
225 "President Donald J. Trump Is Working to Bring Iran's Oil Exports to Zero," The White House, April 22, 2019.
226 Laub and Robinson, "What Is the Status."
227 The White House, "Oil Exports to Zero."
228 World Bank, "Iran Economic Monitor."
229 Thomas Erdbrink, "Already Plagued by Inflation, Iran Is Bracing for Worse," The New York Times, July 1, 2012, sec. World.

Civil servants, like others on fixed salaries, were "reduced to moonlighting in menial jobs" in order to make a living.[230] According to the state-run news agency, over 130,000 workers were not receiving their wages on time as of 2019.[231] Welfare and subsidy programs—from social security and pensions to those relating to health, education. and culture—have been affected as well, despite these typically being priorities for the government to manage levels of public discontent.[232]

Reduction in government revenue from oil arguably has had a more severe impact on ordinary citizens than on funding proxy wars in the Middle East. As articulated by Esfandyar Batmanghelidj, the founder of economic think-tank Bourse and Bazaar, "funding for proxies is by no means dependent on revenues drawn from Iran's legitimate economy, where the ownership of enterprises and assets offers little access to the necessary cash flow and hard currency. For groups such as the IRGC, the real opportunities are in the black market and lucrative smuggling in oil, cash, narcotics, and consumer goods."[233] While Iran's legitimate economy is damaged, the sanctions have had expansionary effects on the black market. When sanctions prohibit Iranian oil from being sold through legitimate means, exporters turn to illegitimate channels.

According to Iran's anti-smuggling agency, $7 billion in petroleum products, including 125,000 barrels of oil per day, were being smuggled out of Iran at the height of the

230 ICHRI, "A Growing Crisis."

231 Mahin Horri, "Why Iran's Workers Are Constantly Protesting to Delayed Payments," People's Mojahedin Organization of Iran (PMOI), August 27, 2019.

232 Dizaji, "The Effects of Oil Shocks."

233 Esfandyar Batmanghelidj, "Tougher U.S. Sanctions Will Enrich Iran's Revolutionary Guards," *Foreign Policy*, October 4, 2018.

international sanctions in 2014—all profits lining the pockets of corrupt elites. In late 2018 Iran's Supreme Economic Coordination Council decided to allow the private purchase of crude oil, in hopes of softening the impact of reimposed sanctions. Though Iran's oil minister Bijan Namdar Zanganeh opposed this action, the government was forced into a difficult decision that likely serves to enrich political rivals and further facilitate the black market.[234] The Iranian government has increasingly been reducing its dependence on oil and gas revenues.[235] Nevertheless, oil profits that are diverted from legitimate channels are a cost to the Iranian public and reduce the government's resources for public programming.

Inflation

For my friend A, the owner of a small electronics store, the surge in inflation from the 2018 sanctions meant soaring prices for their products. Following the announcement of the United States' withdrawal from the JCPOA, Iran's inflation rate skyrocketed. According to A, the Samsung Galaxy J7 that had initially cost 7,000,000 rials rose to as much as 18,000,000 rials in a month. Within three months, the price of the phone had reached 32,000,000 rials—yet in US dollars, all three of these amounts would have translated to around $340.

"It was a disaster," A recounted to me, "Imagine in a really short time everything became at least two times more expensive… A lot of people were struggling for food and clothes, but things like [mobile phones] were not necessary for life;

---

234 Ibid.
235 Katzman, "Iran Sanctions."

[they were] luxuries that a lot of people were deciding not to buy anymore." A was left with no choice but to sell the phones at a lower price that cut into his profit margins, but he still had to pay the shop's rent. The price fluctuation squeezed his business from top and bottom.

Sanctions, along with government mismanagement through subsidies and price regulation, have led to rapid increases in the price of goods. While governments may typically use foreign exchange reserves to prop up the value of its national currency, this option has been rendered unavailable to Iran.[236] Access to Iran's assets abroad is restricted and the Central Bank is prohibited from repatriating hard currency.[237] The quantity of foreign currency available also decreases as oil revenues decrease.[238] Furthermore, to counteract the decrease in spending capacity as a result of diminishing oil exports, the government has been growing the money supply—further driving inflation.[239]

Limited availability of equipment, technology, or other factors of production—i.e. high import costs, as well as the scarcity of certain goods relative to demand—have also contributed to the increasingly exorbitant prices. Iranians who have access to some foreign currency speculate on the price of the rial, causing the economy to be increasingly removed from tangible goods and services. A 2012 *New York Times* article on Iran's dramatic inflation wrote, "In this evolving casino, the winners seize opportunities to make quick

236 Erdbrink, "Already Plagued by Inflation."
237 Katzman, "Iran Sanctions."
238 Navid Kalhor, "Why Iran Could Be Approaching Hyperinflation in Coming Years," Al-Monitor, August 9, 2020.
239 Dalga Khatinoglu, "Government Debt, Deficit, Money Supply Soar, Iran Central Bank Reveals," Radio Farda, February 14, 2020.

money on currency plays, while the losers watch their wealth and savings evaporate almost overnight."[240] To offset inflation, the government tried to subsidize importers of certain essential goods by providing them with lower exchange rates. However, this effectively resulted in a myriad of other issues including corruption and further currency speculation—some of these importers sell the currency back on the market to earn a profit, further driving up inflation.[241]

Given all these inflationary pressures, the poor are disproportionately affected. As of 2018, about a third of the Iranian population lives below the poverty line.[242] Those who are reliant on the domestic economy have seen, at times, the prices of household items such as food and medicine increase by twofold in less than a year. A World Bank report states, "As a consequence of high inflation, the real value of benefits diminished, and this was the key factor behind the increase in poverty."[243] The money people received meant less in terms of purchasing power as the cost of goods went up. For the poorest 20 percent of the Iranian population, cash transfers accounted for almost half of their total income. Thus from 2012-2016 the poverty rate began steadily increasing, erasing more than half of the progress from the previous three years.[244]

Those in the middle class are not safe either. Shortly after the 2018 sanctions, the middle class shrank by 50 percent.[245]

240 Erdbrink, "Already Plagued by Inflation."
241 Leila Gharagozlou, "Inflation Runs Rampant in Tehran as Iran's Government Struggles to Stem Rising Food Prices," CNBC, July 17, 2019.
242 Shahir Shahidsaless, "An Unstable Iran Would Actually Be Very Bad for the US," Middle East Eye, August 30, 2018.
243 World Bank, "Iran Economic Monitor," 38.
244 Ibid.
245 Erdbrink, "Iran's Economic Crisis."

One report from 2013 outlines, "The lower echelons of the middle class have been or are on the verge of being wiped out, and those in the middle are struggling to make ends meet."[246] For Kaveh Tamouri, a college-educated entrepreneur who was starting a family, his monthly income fell from 50 million rials ($1,400) to 10 million rials ($90) within a year because of inflation and currency devaluation. He and his wife had to sell their car, furniture, and wedding gifts as a means of avoiding prison—the punishment that debtors face in a country that enforces Sharia Law.[247]

Tamnoush, a local soda production factory, began incurring significant losses as a consequence of increased import prices for raw materials. After sixteen years of operation, the company had no choice but to shut down, and all forty-five of its workers became jobless. "The men are driving taxis and women are back to being housewives," said the Tamnoush CEO, Farzad Rashidi.[248]

Employment

"From the owner to the line worker, no one is safe... Our country is facing an economic disaster," lamented a manager of rooftop insulation sheets in January 2013.[249]

The manufacturing industry's pre-existing troubles were exacerbated by the effects of 2012 sanctions, to the point where two-thirds of Iran's factories were brought to "the

---

246 Erdbrink, "Already Plagued by Inflation."
247 Erdbrink, "Iran's Economic Crisis."
248 Sharafedin, "Iranian Jobs."
249 ICHRI, "A Growing Crisis", 113.

verge of closure."[250] For those that remained open, most operated at half-capacity. Even before the sanctions started taking full effect, a "sizable proportion" of factories that could have produced substitutes for goods that would no longer be imported under sanctions were already closed or facing imminent closure. Within three years, the bankruptcy rate in Iran had tripled, and 40 percent of men in major cities became newly unemployed over the course of the year.[251]

The employment situation is likely to be worse for women and youth, as they tend to be the first groups to lose their jobs during an economic downturn. In a country where almost half of the population is under thirty, 27 percent of youth are unemployed.[252] What's more, as of 2020, the unemployment rate among those who have obtained higher education is around 20 percent generally, and 30 percent for educated women.[253] Sussan Tahmasebi, director of FEMENA, an organization that supports women human rights defenders, reports, "Hardliners in government use economic problems as an excuse to push women out of work. They often claim that given the poor economic situation, it is better for men to have jobs since, by law, they are recognized as the head of the households."[254]

---

250 Ibid, 13.

251 Ibid, 116.

252 Ahmad Alavi, "Iran's Official Figures Indicate Alarming Unemployment Rate Later This Year," Radio Farda, January 9, 2019.

253 Amin Mohseni-Cheraghlou, "Unemployment Crisis in Iraq and Iran: A Chronic Dilemma for State and Society," Gulf International Forum (blog), March 3, 2020.

254 Medea Benjamin and Sussan Tahmasebi, "Iranian Women Squeezed By US Sanctions, COVID-19 and Their Government," Common Dreams, May 14, 2020.

Business

According to the White House in 2019, foreign direct investment and business activity in Iran have "fallen off" as companies are wary of conducting business in the country. As a result of the "Maximum Pressure" campaign, over 100 companies ceased business relations with Iran.[255] Secondary sanctions have compounded Iran's isolation. Again, not only do sanctions prevent Iran from directly accessing the American financial system, but foreign institutions that make transactions with Iran are also denied access to US dollars—the dominant currency for international trade—for their transactions. Banks have been fined hundreds of millions, and sometimes billions of dollars, for violating US sanctions.[256] The threat of massive fines understandably deters banks and companies from collaborating with their Iranian counterparts. Firms would rather be "over compliant" by avoiding business with Iran, than face the risk of doing anything illegal. Additionally, the time and money required for legal teams to figure out what is permitted in the convoluted sanctions policies often deters companies from engaging with Iranian businesses. Along with those in the US and Europe, banks and companies in South Korea, Taiwan, and Japan have at different points also cut business ties with Iran since sanctions were re-imposed in 2018.[257]

Though the US may have achieved its objective of isolating Iran economically, the domestic humanitarian effects should not be overlooked. Not only does the suspension of foreign direct investment mean the loss of employment

255 The White House, "Oil Exports to Zero."
256 Laub and Robinson, "What Is the Status."
257 "'Maximum Pressure': US Economic Sanctions Harm Iranians' Right to Health," Human Rights Watch, October 29, 2019.

opportunities, but it also means a halt to the transfer of information, technology, and goods. For instance, sanctions affecting the automotive industry have forced more than 300 auto parts manufacturers to terminate production.[258] The short supply of these pieces, in addition to inflation, has made it difficult for taxi drivers to sustain their livelihoods. "My car is my living… If I am not able to maintain it, I won't be able to buy bread," said one such taxi driver during a 2012 interview for the *BBC Persian Service*.[259] Similarly, because of sanctions and the resulting scarcity of auto parts, the cost of production of an automobile increased significantly.[260]

When the French PSA Peugeot Citroën reneged on its 400-million-euro joint venture with Iran Khodro, Iran's largest car manufacturer, Iran attempted to combat the effects of sanctions by contracting domestic manufacturers with the production of auto parts. Even then, only as much as 60 to 85 percent of parts could be produced domestically. Interestingly, although Iran's move may blur some legal boundaries, Peugeot decided to turn a "blind eye," as Khodro's circumvention retained Iranian interest in French vehicles and would benefit Peugeot's "reconquest" of the Iranian market.[261] Nevertheless, the remaining fraction of parts that depended on imports delayed and raised the costs of the entire manufacturing process. For an individual consumer like Leila, an Iranian correspondent interviewed by the International Campaign for Human Rights in Iran, the effects were large: "Not only did they delay delivering my car by three months,

258 Sharafedin, "Iranian Jobs."
259 ICHRI, "A Growing Crisis," 131.
260 Ibid.
261 Elisabeth Studer, "L'Iran demande à ses constructeurs de produire des pièces PSA," *Leblogauto.com* (blog), August 29, 2019.

they also increased the price from 250 million rials to 360 million. Now we have no choice but to pay."[262]

Mori—the man who was lashed for being drunk in public as a teenager—studied mechanical engineering in university. In 2012, he was working in quality control for Iran Khodro. "I remember that time we had problems with many things that needed to be imported... Hundreds of cars were staying at the company and they couldn't give it to people because it wasn't finished yet," he recalled during our interview. "They started making the pieces that they needed by themselves or imported from China, so after that, the quality of the cars became *really* bad—like *bad* bad."

A few years after his stint at the car manufacturer, Mori went into his family business in interior design, specifically working with wood for kitchen setups. He and a former colleague signed a contract to work at an expensive villa belonging to a wealthy man in northern Tehran—but it was right before sanctions were announced. Because inflation made "all the materials" more expensive, the fixed contract cost him his business. "For the whole year working there, I didn't earn anything, and I even lost [money]," said Mori. The wealthy client refused to pay the increased price, and even after a court battle Mori and his colleague were not paid. "If I knew that was going to happen, I would not have signed any contracts... I was really pissed off."

Like Mori, many Iranians have learned their lesson in business and no longer use paperwork. He stated, "Now, when you go to buy something, people don't give you any bill. They say that if we know how much it's going to be tomorrow, you pay us."

---

262 ICHRI, "A Growing Crisis," 131.

Living Under Sanctions

"Sometimes you are two times richer, sometimes you are three times poorer," Koohyar, the tour guide, told me when I asked him about the impact of sanctions. For him, the most "annoying" part of living in a country under sanctions was the unpredictability of the economy, the difficulty of planning for the future, and the resulting sense of insecurity: "I would say it's not delightful to have all these up and downs and to have all these different problems everyday... You cannot plan for the future. In my business for example, you sell a tour six months later, and estimate how much the prices of food cost... And all of a sudden three months later, it becomes much more expensive."

"For a couple of months, it's somehow stable, and then you have a peak of crazy things," Koohyar continued. "Somehow the dollar jumps up, or last year the price of gas became three times more expensive... Suddenly all the taxis increase, and everything increases," he said. People's mentalities have started to adapt to the unpredictability. To Mori, the significant degree of future uncertainty has become "one of the big problems" in Iran. "Making a long-term plan is difficult now," he said. "I don't make a plan for next month, I'm just living for today to see what's happening."

Even without the burden of sanctions, Iran, like many other countries, faced problems of domestic management, as well as other issues like urbanization, modernization, and inequality. For those who are struggling to make ends meet in Iran's current condition, economic sanctions—with the intention of inflicting further damage to Iran's economy—are an additional hurdle in their lives. As articulated by an Iranian reporter, "It is unfair for us [ordinary people] to pay the price of the political squabbling between the two sides [Iran and the West]."[263]

---

263 ICHRI, "A Growing Crisis."

CHAPTER 4

HEALTH

———

"Everyone has the right to a standard of living adequate for the health and well-being of himself and of his family, including food, clothing, housing and medical care and necessary social services."

—ARTICLE 25, THE UNIVERSAL
DECLARATION OF HUMAN RIGHTS[264]

Access to Medical Care in Iran

When my friend M's nephew was born, he suffered from a lack of oxygen to his brain and needed medication for the first two years of his life. However, the medicine was in scarce supply and was only distributed once a month. M, along with the parents of the child, looked everywhere for the medicine—even "asking friends to go to the only

———

264 United Nations, "Universal Declaration of Human Rights."

pharmacy possibly selling that in Tehran." M lived in Isfahan, a five-hour drive from the capital city. Despite everyone's desperate attempts, they could not acquire enough medicine and the infant passed away.

Like most other countries, Iran's life expectancy has steadily increased, and child mortality rates have declined since the 1990s. While long-term statistics suggest generally positive trends in the health of Iranian people, many problems persist and are exacerbated by sanctions. On its own, Iran's healthcare system is "very well developed considering the sanctions imposed on... Iran for many years," yet compared to global developments, "it lags considerably behind" in many aspects.[265]

Given the circumstances, the universal health care system has done relatively well in providing affordable healthcare to Iranian citizens. The government has attempted on several occasions to dampen the effects of sanctions, such as reallocating greater proportions of the budget for healthcare, designating medical supplies as "essential goods," and establishing a heavy subsidy rate for its imports.[266, 267] However, these efforts fail to address inherent problems posed by sanctions, such as the unavailability of foreign goods.

When secondary sanctions prohibit foreign countries from dealing with Iran, the latter loses access to its supply of medical equipment and raw materials to produce medicine. Seventy percent of Iran's medical equipment is imported,

---

265 "Iran Healthcare Sector Analysis 2016-2021—Research and Markets," *India Pharma News*, August 23, 2016.
266 Kokabisaghi, "Assessment of the Effects of Economic Sanctions."
267 "'Maximum Pressure': US Economic Sanctions Harm Iranians' Right to Health," Human Rights Watch, October 29, 2019.

including devices such as MRI machines and hospital beds.[268] Technology to make diagnoses for diseases like cancer are cut off.[269] Cardiac pacemakers go into short supply.[270] Doctors have no choice but to find older anesthetics that are no longer in use because current types can no longer be purchased.[271] Although the heavily subsidized domestic pharmaceutical companies have the capacity to manufacture most medicines consumed in Iran, production is hampered as a third of these drugs require complex raw materials that cannot be sourced domestically.[272] In addition, quality control technologies are not exempt from sanctions and this has had a severe negative effect on the quality of medicines produced in the country.[273]

Medicines that are patented or target rare diseases often have to be imported. Even though imported drugs consist of merely 3 percent of pharmaceuticals consumed in Iran, they have constituted as much as 40 percent and 30 percent of the value of Iran's medical market around the time of sanctions regimes in 2012 and 2018, respectively.[274, 275] The disproportionate ratio of these specific, imported drugs to market share suggests the high demand for these medications and provides a glimpse into the number of Iranian patients affected by sanctions-based restrictions. As of 2014, more than 6 million patients were impacted by medical

---

268 Ibid.

269 Kokabisaghi, "Assessment of the Effects of Economic Sanctions."

270 Bozorgmehr, "Iran Warned."

271 A. Gorji, "Sanctions against Iran: The Impact on Health Services," *Iranian Journal of Public Health* 43, no. 3 (March 2014): 381-82.

272 Human Rights Watch, "Maximum Pressure."

273 Kokabisaghi, "Assessment of the Effects of Economic Sanctions."

274 Ibid.

275 Human Rights Watch, "Maximum Pressure."

shortages.[276] The sanctions regimes have debilitated the Iranian medical system to the extent that at least thirty-two drugs that are "essential" according to the World Health Organization were in short supply pre-JCPOA. This means that by 2016 Iran could not even meet the minimum standards for a functioning healthcare system.[277]

In 2018, the US Special Representative for Iran, Brian Hook, claimed that "every sanctions regime" imposed by the United States "[has made] exceptions for food, medicine, and medical devices."[278] Omitted, however, are the barriers that prevent legal healthcare equipment from being imported to Iran, and the threat of secondary sanctions that prevent banks and businesses from having any relationship with the country. In 2012-2013, the US Office of Foreign Assets Control (OFAC) created the EAR99 "allowed" category for certain medicines and medical devices in an attempt to ease their exportation to Iran. Yet, of the drugs that were reported to experience shortages in 2016, 96 percent of them were EAR99-classified. There were also the Non-EAR99 pharmaceuticals that required additional controls and were thus even harder to export. These included items like vaccines, medical supplies, devices, and chemicals, because they were feared to be used for non-medical, weapon-related purposes.[279]

Bank overcompliance, restricted financing options for Iran, and the devaluation of the rial are primary causes of the supply restriction. For banks, the threat of hundreds of

---

276 Gorji, "Sanctions against Iran."

277 Sogol Setayesh and Tim K. Mackey, "Addressing the Impact of Economic Sanctions on Iranian Drug Shortages in the Joint Comprehensive Plan of Action: Promoting Access to Medicines and Health Diplomacy," *Globalization and Health* 12, no. 1 (June 8, 2016): 31.

278 U.S. Embassy in Georgia, "Iran Sanctions/Europe."

279 Setayesh and Mackey, "Addressing the Impact of Economic Sanctions."

millions of dollars in fines from US secondary sanctions is too costly to risk a transaction. When a senior Iranian pharmaceutical representative flew to Paris in 2012 to provide evidence on the legality of the proposed trade with the French bank, he was told: "Even if you bring a letter from the French president himself saying it is OK to do so, we will not risk this."[280]

This risk-averse attitude from banks has been well-documented globally, both pre- and post-JCPOA. In 2012, a patented American drug that prevents the body from rejecting an organ transplant could not fulfill an order from Iran because of "sanctions-related banking complications."[281] In 2019, a European company producing medical dressing for patients with a skin condition called epidermolysis bullosa (EB) "decided not to conduct any business with relation to Iran," further clarifying that this refusal "also applies to business conducted under any form of exemptions to the US economic sanctions."[282, 283] The Swiss Banque de Commerce et de Placements (BCP), which had previously engaged in humanitarian-related dealings with Iran, also decided to suspend "all new business in Iran" when the reimposition of sanctions was announced in May 2018.[284] The concerns of these firms are not unfounded, as the US Treasury Department has a precedent of prosecuting pharmaceutical companies for selling "small amounts of medical supplies" to Iran.[285]

---

280 Namazi, "Sanctions and Medical Supply Shortages."
281 Siamak Namazi, "Sanctions and Medical Supply Shortages in Iran," *Wilson Center*, Viewpoints No. 20, February 2013, 12.
282 Namazi, "Sanctions and Medical Supply Shortages."
283 Human Rights Watch, "Maximum Pressure."
284 Namazi, "Sanctions and Medical Supply Shortages."
285 Sina Azodi, "How US Sanctions Hinder Iranians' Access to Medicine," *Atlantic Council* (blog), May 31, 2019.

Nevertheless, Iranian people are the ones who ultimately bear the burden of these consequences: the patient who has waited years for an organ donor now lacks post-transplant medication; the girl with EB that has to endure "excruciating pain" because the only available low-quality dressing often gets attached to the blisters on her skin.[286]

When I asked Mori whether sanctions have affected his experience of the healthcare system, he recounted his search for the flu vaccine. "I wanted to get the influenza vaccine for my [elderly] parents," he said. "But I couldn't find any vaccine in Iran. [The government] said we would get the vaccine soon, but we didn't see anything in the pharmacies... My brother is a doctor, and he couldn't find it."

Manouchehr, a fifteen-year-old boy from southwestern Iran, died of hemophilia.[287] This condition, where the body is unable to properly form blood clots, causes the sufferer to bleed severely from the smallest injuries. Although there is currently no cure for this genetic condition, expensive treatments that involve lifelong injections multiple times a week are available to stop the bleeding.[288] Because import restrictions had reduced Iran's stock of hemophilia medicine down to a third, Manouchehr lost access to the US and European-made medicine that allowed him to live.[289]

Sanctions regimes' restrictions on currency trading and the inaccessibility of Iranian assets abroad make it difficult for the government to pay for mass orders of medical

---

286 Human Rights Watch, "Maximum Pressure."

287 Saeed Kamali Dehghan, "Haemophiliac Iranian Boy 'Dies after Sanctions Disrupt Medicine Supplies,'" *The Guardian*, November 14, 2012, sec. World news.

288 Catharine Paddock, "Hemophilia Cure? Gene Therapy Trial Shows Dramatic Results," *Medical News Today*, December 15, 2017.

289 Dehghan, "Haemophiliac Iranian Boy."

imports. Due to the relentlessness of the sanctions regime, firms have lost confidence in taking Iranian debt.[290] Orders from Iran for medical equipment therefore have to be paid in advance, in cash.[291] By 2016, approximately $115 billion in Iran's hard currency reserves were frozen abroad. When access was granted through sanctions relief between 2016 and 2018, most of that money remained abroad as a way to pay for imports.[292] However, when these funds are restricted under sanctions, it becomes extremely difficult for Iran to obtain dollars or euros. While Iranian banks may still have access to rupees, won, yuan, or even Turkish lira, American and European pharmaceutical companies do not accept these currencies, adding a further obstacle to the purchase of medical supplies.[293] According to the Wilson Center, the pre-JCPOA sanctions decreased medical imports by 30 percent, and in 2013 pharmaceutical imports from the US to Iran were reduced by half.[294]

The devaluation of the rial has made medicine significantly more expensive and decreased Iran's purchasing ability. Inflation in healthcare reached as high as 44.3 percent and 45.6 percent in cities and rural regions in 2012.[295] As of 2019, the overall inflation rate has reached levels comparable to what it was in 2012, suggesting that inflation for the medical sector is likely similar.[296, 297] Pharmaceutical exports to Iran

---

290 Namazi, "Sanctions and Medical Supply Shortages."
291 Kokabisaghi, "Assessment of the Effects of Economic Sanctions."
292 Katzman, "Iran Sanctions."
293 Namazi, "Sanctions and Medical Supply Shortages."
294 Setayesh and Mackey, "Addressing the Impact of Economic Sanctions."
295 Kokabisaghi, "Assessment of the Effects of Economic Sanctions."
296 Ibid.
297 "'Maximum Pressure': US Economic Sanctions Harm Iranians' Right to Health," Human Rights Watch, October 29, 2019.

are "significantly higher" in cost than for neighboring Pakistan, who does not face unilateral sanctions but has a similar economy.[298] Moreover, Iranian insurance companies have had to decrease their coverage as a result of the increased expenses, causing those who are unable to pay to become dependent on risky self-treatment.[299]

For the average Iranian citizen, all these obstacles amount to insurmountable trouble in obtaining adequate medical care. Mohammed, a boy from a southern neighborhood of Tehran with a condition that makes him too weak to carry his backpack, is believed to have a rare genetic disease. However, because sanctions have caused the costs of genetic testing to triple within a year to the point where it has become unaffordable for Mohammed's family, the boy has not been able to receive a diagnosis for his condition.[300] Mohammed's mother told the BBC, "I asked the doctor, how am I supposed to pay that money? He said, 'I don't know, I'm just like you.'" Every year, 1 percent of the Iranian population falls below the poverty line as a result of "catastrophic health expenditures."[301] People turn to black markets for any medicine they can get, paying as much as four times the market price for medications that are unsafe and probably expired.[302]

298 Ibid.
299 Kokabisaghi, "Assessment of the Effects of Economic Sanctions."
300 BBC News, "Six Charts."
301 Kokabisaghi, "Assessment of the Effects of Economic Sanctions."
302 Dara Mohammadi, "US-Led Economic Sanctions Strangle Iran's Drug Supply," The Lancet 381, no. 9863 (January 26, 2013): 279.

Humanitarian Banking Channels and Foreign Aid

In late 2019, the US and Swiss governments worked on establishing a humanitarian banking channel that would facilitate Iran's purchase of aid such as medicine, food, and other supplies from Swiss companies and prevent the Iranian government from diverting funds from its people. However, as of July 2020, Iran's Central Bank has been unable to transfer billions of dollars made from oil revenues during the JCPOA era to banks working with the humanitarian channel.[303]

Iran's access to its own funds is essential for the operation of this banking facility, and thereby Iranian people's access to humanitarian goods. According to the Swiss State Secretariat for Economic Affairs (SECO), the banking channel required "regular transfers of Iranian funds from abroad for its functioning" and these transactions were "support[ed]" by the US. So far, only one Swiss bank has agreed to accept payments from Iran through this banking channel.[304]

Because these funds had been frozen when sanctions were reimposed, international banks have struggled to receive all the authorizations necessary to move them. Banks—who are already risk-averse to heavy fines for violating sanctions—have to seek permission from their governments, which in turn require clearance from the US There is also the obstacle of insurance and shipping companies, who are "unwilling to provide vessels or cover for voyages, even for approved commerce."[305]

---

303 Jonathan Saul, Ana Mano, and Joori Roh, "Iran Struggles to Buy Food in a World Wary of Touching Its Money," *Reuters*, July 30, 2020.

304 Ibid.

305 Ibid.

According to a *Reuters* article about sanctions affecting Iran's food and medical supplies in 2020, a South Korean foreign ministry official stated, "Any permission regarding the funds need to be strictly authorized by the US." And when this person was asked about the possibility of clearing Iran's cash revenue through the Swiss channel, the official replied that the "US hasn't been positive about such proposals."[306] The American government's hindrance to these transactions is reflected by an anonymous Iranian official: "These countries have approached the US to secure its approval for such a transfer, but to no avail."[307]

Although the US Treasury announced in January 2020 that initial transactions through this humanitarian banking channel had been "successful," six months later this no longer seemed to be the case—at least to the extent that might have been anticipated.[308]

Coronavirus

Iran is one of the countries hardest hit with the coronavirus pandemic. Its total number of deaths reached as high as 29,000, as of October 2020.[309] During the crisis, many public officials—including the World Health Organization (WHO), four former NATO secretaries-general, former US and European politicians, human rights groups, and a group

---

306 Ibid.

307 Ibid.

308 "United States Announces Successful Initial Transactions Through Humanitarian Channel for Iran," U.S. Department of the Treasury, January 30, 2020.

309 "Coronavirus Update (Live)," Worldometer, last updated October 22, 2020.

of US Senators—have all advocated for sanctions relief.[310, 311] The group of Senators wrote a letter stating, "US sanctions are hindering the free flow of desperately needed medical and humanitarian supplies due to the broad chilling effect of sanctions on such transactions, even when there are technical exemptions."[312] Yet other hawkish American officials urged sanctions to continue, viewing the additional pressure from the pandemic as making Iran more likely to "capitulate to US demands."[313]

Iranian and American governments have publicly displayed hostility to one another in the midst of the pandemic. Though Iran did receive aid from more than thirty countries to fight the COVID crisis between February and March 2020, it rejected the United States' offers of "unconditional" aid, arguing that rather than sending in supplies, easing sanctions would enable Iran to handle the situation itself. The Iranian government also expressed distrust in Washington's leadership.[314, 315, 316] At the same time, Iran, desperate for aid, requested an emergency loan of $5 billion from the International Monetary Fund (IMF) for the first time since

---

310 Marc Champion and Golnar Motevalli, "How Iran's Virus Fight Is Tied to Struggle With U.S.," *Bloomberg*, August 3, 2020.

311 Gareth Smyth, "How a Misleading Report on Iran from a Hawkish 'Think Tank' Made Its Way to Trump Administration Talking Points," *Responsible Statecraft* (blog), April 22, 2020.

312 Christopher S. Murphy and et al. to Hon. Michael Pompeo and Hon. Steven Mnuchin, March 26, 2020.

313 Champion and Motevalli, "Iran's Virus Fight."

314 "Dozens of Countries Send COVID-19 Aid to Iran," United States Institute of Peace: The Iran Primer, last updated April 29, 2020.

315 Champion and Motevalli, "Iran's Virus Fight."

316 Reuters Editorial, "Iran Rejects U.S. Offer of Coronavirus Help," Reuters, August 26, 2020.

1962—and was blocked by the US.[317] The United States claimed the move was to prevent Iran from diverting the IMF funds to be used in other parts of its economy or to fund its regional aggression.[318]

Regardless of reasons claimed by both countries, it is clear that the antagonistic US-Iran relations, and the sanctions issue in particular, has politicized Iran's situation to the extent that Iranian people are robbed of potential aid as a consequence of geopolitics. "While the coronavirus outbreak could have provided Tehran and Washington an opportunity to cooperate against a common foe, the enmity and mistrust between them has proven too wide for even a deadly pandemic to bridge," wrote Karim Sadjadpour for the Carnegie Endowment for International Peace.[319]

Moreover, while the extent to which sanctions have impacted Iran's ability to manage the pandemic is unclear, it is generally agreed that Iran's healthcare system has been damaged by economic sanctions. Thus, the relatively low existing capacity of medical facilities likely contributed to Iran's poor capacity to deal with the crisis. Besides, many general medical supplies and equipment that face import barriers (like decontamination equipment and full-mask respirators) also required special licenses under sanctions guidelines. Yet whereas half of all license requests were approved in 2016, by 2019, the US Treasury Department only approved 10 percent of medical device exports that require these licenses.[320]

---

317 Karim Sadjadpour, "Iran's Coronavirus Disaster," Carnegie Endowment for International Peace, March 25, 2020.

318 Ian Talley and Benoit Faucon, "U.S. to Block Iran's Request to IMF for $5 Billion Loan to Fight Coronavirus," *Wall Street Journal*, April 7, 2020, sec. World.

319 Sadjadpour, "Iran's Coronavirus Disaster."

320 Smyth, "Misleading Report on Iran."

Five authors from London and Tehran for the British medical journal, *The Lancet*, in April 2020 wrote, "Even before COVID-19, Iran's health system was feeling the effect of the sanctions. Their impact is now severe because they restrict the government's ability to raise funds or to import essential goods.[321] Consequently, although approximately 184,000 hospital and primary health-care staff were working to fight COVID-19, their efforts were thwarted by shortages of test kits, protective equipment, and ventilators. WHO has provided crucial supplies, sufficient equipment for 31,000 workers, but supplies are still substantially short of what is needed."[322]

***

Economic sanctions have restricted Iranian people's access to medicine and healthcare. Moreover, it has made people's right to health and wellbeing a political issue. The lives of Iranian citizens are in the hands of politicians and government officials who, without sufficient regard for humanitarian consequences, deny access to aid and reject requests to export life-saving medical equipment. If M's family had access to medication, his nephew might be a toddler now; the fifteen-year-old boy, Manouchehr, might not have died of hemophilia. Though the casualties of economic warfare may be less visible or dramatic than those in a military war, they are not any less real or devastating and deserve to be recognized.

---

321 Adrianna Murphy et al., "Economic Sanctions and Iran's Capacity to Respond to COVID-19," The Lancet Public Health 5, no. 5 (May 2020): e254.

322 Ibid.

CHAPTER 5

FOOD

——

Overview

When I asked my friend Nicolas what stood out to him about Iranian cuisine, he replied: "A lot of saffron."

"The rice was good," he added, "saffron made it good."

Iran's traditional food bears elements from ancient Greece and Rome and other Asian and Mediterranean cuisines.[323] Many Persian dishes are similar to those found in Turkish and Indian cuisines, although each country would say that they were the originators. Saffron, basil, mint, cumin, coriander, pistachio, and pomegranate are just some of the many colorful ingredients that can be found in Iranian food. A typical meal consists of rice, meats, bread, and vegetables, although ingredients and style of cooking vary from region to region.

Certain traditional foods remain the same, such as Javaher Polow ("Jeweled Rice"), which looks like the name

---

323 Massoume Price, "Persian Cuisine, a Brief History," Culture of Iran, October 2009.

suggests: brightly colored dried fruits and nuts are embedded into saffron rice, including pistachios, almonds, pomegranate candied orange peel, barberries, and carrots.[324, 325] But like the rest of the world and in spite of its economic isolation, the daily dietary habits of Iranians have been changing as the country undergoes modernization. Koohyar described to me that, "People used to eat a lot at home, but now the younger generation—people like me—are spending a lot more time eating outside. It's not like the old traditional meal with kebab barbecues or skewers. Now it's more like burgers with French fries and that kind of stuff." Coca-Cola and Pepsi are now "ubiquitous" in Iran.[326, 327]

Although international chains like McDonald's or Pizza Hut do not engage in business with Iran (though there had been McDonald's restaurants in Iran prior to the 1979 revolution), there have been a variety of local fast-food alternatives. Some are even named Mash Donald's, Pizza Hot, and Sheak Shack.[328, 329] Iran is no stranger to "Walmartization," wherein chain restaurants take over smaller, local businesses.[330] "We used to have a lot of local supermarkets, but now we start to

---

324 Louisa Shafia, "Persian Food Primer: 10 Essential Iranian Dishes," *Food Republic* (blog), October 29, 2014.

325 Azita Mehran, "Turmeric & Saffron: Javaher Polow—Persian Jeweled Rice," *Turmeric & Saffron* (blog), January 10, 2011.

326 Thomas Erdbrink, "Iran Capitalizing on a Taste for America's Biggest Brands (Published 2015)," *The New York Times*, August 2, 2015, sec. World.

327 Jon Gambrell, "Some Iranians Embrace American Culture with a Coke and a Smile," *Christian Science Monitor*, July 11, 2019.

328 Sarra Sedghi, "How Bootleg Fast Food Conquered Iran," Atlas Obscura, March 29, 2018.

329 Shaahin Pishbin, "The Best Fast Food Spots In Tehran," Culture Trip, September 27, 2016.

330 Jayson Demers, "Small Business Growth Has Stalled and That's Bad for All of Us," Time, March 23, 2017.

have a lot of chain supermarkets," said Koohyar. The same goes for restaurants: "… from small little sandwich shops or falafel shops in the neighborhood to big chains… brands are booming, and people are starting to care more about [where] they are eating," he continued. For the modern Iranian pressed for time, even traditional Sangak bread comes packaged and mass-produced. As Nicolas observed, the store-bought version was identifiable by its "square marks" and found "literally everywhere".

In addition to modernization in the sense of chain restaurants and packaged foods, there has also been a movement towards healthier eating and vegetarianism, as people become increasingly aware of health and social consequences.[331] "People are starting to think more about nature, health," said Koohyar, "and now we have vegan and vegetarian restaurants." Even the owner of Mash Donald's, Hassan, prefers to eat at home: "fast food makes you super fat," he said.[332]

But at the same time as some Iranian people in the cities may be experiencing some of the global food trends shaping the modern world, there is a growing number of middle and working-class Iranian people who face problems of adequate nutrition. Food remains generally available in supermarkets—abundance is not really the issue. Rather, grocery item prices have become increasingly unaffordable to a large portion of the population.

As of June 2020, the income needed in a four-person household to be above the poverty line had increased by 80 percent within two years to 45 million rials per month (roughly $250)—above the monthly minimum wage of 30

---

331 "Iranians Forced to Forgo Meat Staples as Prices Soar," Bourse & Bazaar, May 9, 2019.
332 Erdbrink, "Iran Capitalizing."

million rials (~$200) for most ordinary workers and laborers.[333] As of 2017, about 10-12 million Iranian people live under the poverty line. Millions are likely to have joined this group since the economic downturn began in 2018 when sanctions were reimposed.[334]

Nutrition

When the sanctions were re-imposed following the US exit from the JCPOA, the price of beef skyrocketed from 380,000 rials per kilogram to almost 1.2 million rials per kilo within three months.[335] A Tehran taxi driver described his loss of purchasing power as going to "a jewelry shop when I go to a butchers."[336]

Others complained that they have not been able to purchase meat for months. According to Ramin, the owner of a small butcher shop in an affluent neighborhood of Tehran, customers who used to purchase "at least five kilos of beef a month" have more than halved their purchases. "There are even those who have completely removed meat from their baskets, buying only bones just to have a flavor of meat in their cooking." Those with even fewer means to begin with were being "squeezed," as the economic impacts disproportionately harm the poor.[337] A shopkeeper in a lower-mid-

---

333 Radio Farda, "As Cost Of Living Rises In Iran Millions Fall Under Poverty Line," Radio Farda, June 5, 2020.

334 Radio Farda, "As Cost Of Living Rises."

335 Gharagozlou, "Inflation Runs Rampant."

336 Najmeh Bozorgmehr, "Iran Warned on Food Security," Financial Times, April 3, 2013.

337 Bourse & Bazaar, "Iranians Forced to Forgo Meat."

dle-class neighborhood agreed with these sentiments: "[B]efore, people who could not afford to eat meat were at least having bread and yoghurt. But now even yoghurt is becoming unaffordable for some families."[338]

Since the 2010-2013 sanctions, the government has attempted to decrease spending by cutting some of its subsidies on bread and other essential items. However, this may have made life more difficult for poor Iranians, who are increasingly dissatisfied with both the economy and the government's response to it—as reflected by the recent waves of protests.[339]

Inflation and decreased government revenues as a result of the sanctions regime negatively affected food subsidies and welfare programs. In addition, sanctions on the Iranian financial sector "effectively frustrate[d] the purpose behind humanitarian exceptions," as food imports had to be processed by foreign banks and often caused payment issues.[340, 341] The prices of essential goods such as cooking oil, fruit, vegetables, meats, and nuts rose sharply.[342]

"If you go to the supermarket and you want to buy something, you'll see that within one week it got 10 percent more expensive. And it's an Iranian product," said Mori. "Normal people these days are getting poorer."

---

338 Najmeh Bozorgmehr and Monavar Khalaj, "Poor Iranians Bear Brunt of Sanctions as Food Prices Soar," *Financial Times*, August 6, 2018.

339 Ibid.

340 United Nations High Commissioner for Refugees (UNHCR), "Situation of Human Rights in the Islamic Republic of Iran : Note / by the Secretary-General," Refworld, October 4, 2013.

341 C Joy Gordon, "Crippling Iran: The UN Security Council and the Tactic of Deliberate Ambiguity," *Georgetown Journal of International Law* 44, no. 3 (2013): 973-1006.

342 UNHCR, "Situation of Human Rights."

Food prices tripled within a year of the US announcement of JCPOA withdrawal.[343] By August 2018, the inflation on food prices had reached the highest point experienced in four years, at 36 percent.[344] Fruit and nuts cost almost twice as much as before, and the price of vegetables and beans have continued to increase—up to 48 percent within the month of December 2019.[345, 346] Wheat, corn, raw sugar, and other imports halted as food traders no longer saw "[any] real chance of being paid."[347] Although prices may have doubled in rial, the currency devaluation against the dollar has been so significant that one man recounted to me the cost of meat actually decreasing in dollars—$15 per kilo then versus $8 in 2020.

High food prices often do not benefit domestic producers either. Because sanctions have impeded imports, products that include more expensive imported components have to be charged at a higher price. In part because tuna cans have to be assembled abroad, the price of tuna rose from 25,000 rials to 190,000 rials. Similarly, packaging for dairy products is also imported, and their prices have almost doubled.[348, 349] Most consumers cannot afford such exorbitant prices and many suppliers have gone out of business.[350] As of 2011, approximately a third of the Iranian population "could

---

343 World Bank, "Iran Economic Monitor."

344 Ibid.

345 Ibid.

346 "Food Price Inflation In Iran At 30 Percent According To Latest Report," Radio Farda, January 20, 2020.

347 Jonathan Saul and Parisa Hafezi, "Exclusive: Global Traders Halt New Iran Food Deals as U.S. Sanctions Bite—Sources," *Reuters*, December 21, 2018.

348 ICHRI, "A Growing Crisis."

349 Saeed Kamali Dehghan, "Iranian Baby Milk Shortage Blamed on Sanctions," *The Guardian*, November 6, 2012, sec. World news.

350 Gharagozlou, "Inflation Runs Rampant."

not afford to eat enough," and the number is likely to have increased since then. Due to the divergence between the price sold and consumers' purchasing power, the Dairy Industries Union remarked that dairy consumption had decreased by 30 percent within the year of 2013.[351] Many businesses selling tuna have also closed.[352] As sanctions have prevented domestic companies from selling to other countries, businesses cannot look for external sources of demand, further hindering agricultural growth.[353]

For those with dietary restrictions, the combination of high prices and low import supplies becomes even more of a challenge. Special milk powder for babies with allergies or dietary restrictions cannot be produced domestically, and under the first round of sanctions in 2011, its price had increased fourteen-fold.[354] An infant girl who had diarrhea did not receive the special formula necessary to treat her illness. She was hospitalized as a result, recovering "using medicine and serum," as her mother recounted. "What should I do when my baby is crying from hunger?" asked another new mother.[355]

In preparation for the new round of post-JCPOA sanctions in 2018, the government had stocked up for ten months' worth of special milk formula and distributed it at subsidized prices. Yet because the public had witnessed the shortage for special formula only seven years earlier, they flocked to

---

351 Bozorgmehr, "Iran Warned."
352 Gharagozlou, "Inflation Runs Rampant."
353 IFP Editorial Staff, "Iran Producing $80 Billion Worth of Agricultural Products," *Iran Front Page* (blog), October 23, 2019.
354 Mohammadi, "US-Led Economic Sanctions."
355 Nikki Mahjoub, "Iranian 'hungry' babies waiting for powdered milk," *BBC Persian* (October 30, 2012).

hoard the regular formula—emptying a two-month stockpile in four days.[356]

Burdens of accessibility have changed Iranian's relationship with food. While their traditional diets typically consist of a variety of wheat, fruits, and vegetables, people increasingly consume fewer fruits and vegetables (as well as meat), as they have "become too expensive."[357] According to a 2013 Gallup Poll, 50 percent of Iranians experienced "not hav[ing] enough money to buy the food [they] or [their] family needed" at some point within the past year.[358] As a result, food inadequacy has been increasing.[359]

For many people, the sanctions' effects on food prices meant a return to more basic concerns of food security. The nutritional values of Iranians' consumption baskets "plummeted" due to a decline in purchasing power, exposing them to risks of nutrient deficiency and illness. In these conditions, even clothing becomes a luxury as money is redirected to purchasing food, as was the case for Golnaz, a government employee. Despite having worked at a stable job for forty years, she was barely able to afford meat, and some of her colleagues had resorted to eating "plain pasta." Although official statistics in late 2012 suggested 3.75 million hungry people in Iran, this number is most likely an underestimate and would have risen throughout the sanctions period, and omits an even greater population of malnourished individuals.[360]

356 Mohammadi, "US-Led Economic Sanctions."
357 Soazic Heslot, "Iran's Food Security," *Future Directions International* (blog), August 8, 2014.
358 Steve Crabtree, "Half of Iranians Lack Adequate Money for Food, Shelter," Gallup, July 1, 2013.
359 David Michel, "Iran's Troubled Quest for Food Self-Sufficiency," *Atlantic Council* (blog), July 9, 2019.
360 ICHRI, "A Growing Crisis."

More recent data after sanctions were reimposed in 2018 does not yet seem to be available.

Malnutrition often comes in the form of overnutrition (leading to obesity) or undernutrition (leading to nutrient deficiencies). While there is a lack of sufficient data on certain nutritional indicators, such as childhood stunting and birth weight, evidence has shown increasingly worrying trends of malnutrition in the country. Around 65 percent of the Iranian population is obese or overweight, while indicators such as anemia in women of reproductive age (which suggests micronutrient deficiencies), diabetes, and childhood obesity have also been increasing significantly.[361, 362, 363] Yet, Iranians' salt intake fall short of the global average.[364] With nutritional options such as fruits, meats, and vegetables becoming increasingly inaccessible to a greater proportion of the population, these statistics are likely to worsen.

Understandably, Iranian people adapt to supply shortages or further price increases by hoarding essential products. This mentality is described by Nasrin, a new mother in Tehran: "I used to buy two or three [cans of baby formula], but when I heard that it was scarce, I bought twenty cans, and when it ran out, it could not be found."[365] In attempts to regulate basic food items, the government controls the distribution of sugar to supermarkets and has set its official price at 38,000 to 40,000 rials. Often found in excess in the

---

361 "Iran (Islamic Republic of) Nutrition Profile," Global Nutrition Report, accessed October 22, 2020.

362 "65% of Iranian Population Overweight, Obese," Tehran Times, December 23, 2018.

363 "'Childhood Obesity Rate Worryingly Soars in Iran,'" Tehran Times, March 16, 2019.

364 Global Nutrition Report, "Iran."

365 Mahjoub, "Iranian 'hungry' babies."

US, sugar has become a "luxury item" to Iranians. To stock up on sugar, people wait in lines for as long as ten hours before an expected shipment. However, many return home empty-handed as the supply could not satisfy all those who had waited. Those who are desperate may be willing to spend as much as three to five times the official rate, out of fear that the price may continue to rise.[366]

Nevertheless, not all domestic problems related to food scarcity issues are due to sanctions. Government mismanagement and distorted incentives for corruption and profiteering have contributed to the issue while failing to stem the soaring prices. Because certain companies are granted artificially low exchange rates to stimulate import of essential goods, importers are able to profit from the price difference of the high free-market rates of these items and the artificially low import prices—sometimes using the favorable rate to import altogether different items with higher margins. Not only have they found lucrative businesses selling goods on the Iranian free market, but some have even started smuggling livestock and food products into neighboring countries like Iraq, where they have been able to double their investment. Misuse of government-allocated subsidized currency to profit in foreign markets has aggravated shortages within the country. Companies have also been caught storing warehouses full of food products—waiting to cash in on price fluctuations, thereby worsening pricing and supply conditions.[367]

***

366 Gharagozlou, "Inflation Runs Rampant."
367 Bourse & Bazaar, "Iranians Forced to Forgo Meat."

Sanctions, in combination with domestic factors like governance, has led to supply shortages and price fluctuations of essential food items. Against the backdrop of Iran's vibrant traditional cuisine that consists of saffron, pistachio, pomegranate, fresh meat and vegetables, ordinary people— including those living in middle-class neighborhoods in Tehran—have "resorted to buying withered cucumbers and rotting tomatoes, grapes, apples and peaches that grocery store salesmen put aside every day at dusk."[368] For more vulnerable populations such as the young and the poor, it means risking malnutrition, malnourishment, and even hunger. As the next chapter will show, the issue of affordability on food and nutrition is only one part of the problem. While there is a daily issue of meals, there is also the longer-term problem of managing a decent living situation.

---

368 Ramin Mostaghim and Melissa Etehad, "Middle-Class Iranians Resort to Buying Rotting Produce as U.S. Sanctions Take Toll," *Los Angeles Times*, August 28, 2019, sec. World & Nation.

CHAPTER 6

ENVIRONMENT

___

Environmental Damage

"If nothing changes in the coming years, more than half of Iran's provinces will have to evacuate. They'll simply become unlivable."

—THOMAS ERDBRINK IN HIS VIDEO, "THE EMPTY RIVER OF LIFE," FOR *THE NEW YORK TIMES*[369]

Water

As the eighteenth largest country in the world by area, Iran experiences a range of climates: temperatures can range from -20°C (-4°F) in the northwest to above 55°C (131°F) in

___

369 Thomas Erdbrink, "Video: The Empty River of Life," *The New York Times,* May 5, 2015, sec. World.

the southwest; central and southeastern regions may have less than 50 mm of rain in a year, but coastal regions may experience more than 1,600 mm of rainfall annually.[370, 371] Nevertheless, the majority of Iran is arid or semiarid.[372] Most rainfall occurs in a small section of the country, while the rest of the land (about 65 percent) receives less than 100 mm of annual rainfall—for context, deserts on average receive 250 mm of rain per year.[373, 374] Because of the natural scarcity of water in many regions, early civilizations in Iran developed methods of water management. For instance, the ancient qanat system that transferred groundwater using kilometers of underground tunnels was constructed as early as 2,500 to 3,000 years ago.[375] Designated by the UN as a Globally Important Agricultural Heritage System, it once made Iran "the most fertile area in the history of Asia."[376, 377]

Yet in the modern era, Iran's water availability has diminished. In less than fifty years, Iran has depleted around 70 percent of its groundwater supply.[378] Based on the high usage of water relative to what is available as calculated by the

370 "Largest Countries in the World by Area," Worldometer, accessed October 22, 2020.

371 Masoud Saatsaz, *A Historical Investigation on Water Resources Management in Iran*, 2019.

372 Ibid.

373 Ibid.

374 "Desert," NASA Earth Observatory (NASA Earth Observatory, October 22, 2020).

375 "Qanāt," Encyclopedia Britannica, accessed October 22, 2020.

376 UNESCO World Heritage Centre, "The Persian Qanat," UNESCO World Heritage Centre, accessed October 22, 2020.

377 Ding Gang, "Self-Sufficiency Helps Iran Counter Sanctions," Global Times, May 15, 2019.

378 Kayla Ritter, "Tehran Faces Crisis As Iran's Water Supply Runs Low," *Circle of Blue* (blog), June 6, 2018.

Criticality Ratio, Iran falls in the category of a "high water stress region."[379] The World Resources Institute similarly ranks Iran as the fourth most water-stressed country globally.[380] At current rates of depletion, 50 million Iranians are at risk of forced migration if current farming practices and water consumption continue.[381] Moreover, desertification has already led to increased soil erosion as well as changes in animal habitats and migration patterns.[382] Because of increased drought, "many species of plants have died," according to Isa Kalantari, the head of Iran's Department of Environment. "That has impacted the population of rabbits and black-tailed gazelle which graze in the grasslands. As a result, the number of predators that feed on these herbivores has sharply dropped."[383]

Deadly dust storms have been recorded to occur at higher frequencies as a result of "changes in land and water use."[384] These dust storms—a consequence of desertification—have brought high winds that cause damage to trees and power lines, as well as the suspension of dust particles in the air which, when inhaled, increase the risk of pulmonary diseases and cancer.[385] Due to instances of "severe air pollution,"

379 Saatsaz, *A Historical Investigation*.
380 Austin Bodetti, "Iran Struggles With Food Security Amid Sanctions," LobeLog, September 16, 2019.
381 Connor Dilleen, "Will Renewed US Sanctions Worsen Iran's Water Security Crisis?," The Strategist—The Australian Strategic Policy Institute (ASPI), August 7, 2018.
382 "Hamoun Wetlands: Current Situation and the Way Forward" (United Nations Development Program (UNDP), March 2014).
383 Fardine Hamidi, trans., "Iran's Zagros Mountains Face Water Shortage, Threatening Wildlife, Plants," Khayan Life, February 24, 2019.
384 Richard Angwin, "Dust Storms—a Modern Plague on Iran," Al Jazeera, June 4, 2014.
385 "Residents Abandoning Regions With Increasingly Fierce Sandstorms," Radio Farda, April 30, 2018.

schools, government offices, and businesses have closed.[386] People have already been leaving their homes in Khuzestan province in southwestern Iran because the storms have been so disruptive to their lives—in 2018, 235 days of the year were determined to have "unhealthy weather."[387] These dust storms have even reached Tehran, where school closures have become a "winter routine" due to air pollution.[388] The independent news agency Radio Farda wrote, "Though the exact cause of the increase in storms is not known, accelerated dam construction and diversion of water resources for agriculture throughout the region is thought to be the main culprit."[389]

Since the 1979 revolution, Iran has adopted the objective of being completely food self-reliant as a means of becoming less dependent on Western imports. This policy has continued throughout the Iran-Iraq war to today, as the enduring antagonism between Iran and the international community threatens its food security.[390] When American sanctions were reimposed in 2018, banking systems became "paralyzed," impeding transactions between Iran and other countries. By the end of that year, foreign food suppliers such as Cargill, Incorporated, Bunge Limited, and Olam International from the US and Singapore had suspended their exports to Iran.[391] As a comparison, Iran in 2017 had imported 1.2 million metric tons of rice, 1.3 million tons of barley, and 9.5 million

---

386 Angwin, "Dust Storms."

387 Radio Farda, "Residents Abandoning Regions."

388 Tom Lewis and Kaveh Madani, "End of Sanctions May Help Iran Face an Accelerating Environmental Crisis," *The Guardian*, January 20, 2016, sec. World news.

389 Radio Farda, "Residents Abandoning Regions."

390 Saatsaz, *A Historical Investigation*.

391 Saul and Hafezi, "Exclusive: Global Traders."

tons of corn.[392] Although thus far food remains relatively available (but at high prices) in Iran, the threat of not having enough food supply is real and present. Iran's objective of agricultural self-sufficiency is therefore as important as ever to build resistance to food import fluctuations. According to Mohammad Bakhshoodeh, head of the agricultural economics department at Shiraz University in 2019:

> "To keep national food security, the Iranian government focuses on self-sufficiency policies, concentrates on domestic production of food and other agricultural products, and encourages productivity enhancement of basic inputs, particularly that of water. Moreover, the government supports farmers with policies of guaranteeing purchases, expanding agricultural insurances with significant coverage, and so on."[393]

Iran's sanctions-resistance strategy might make sense in theory, but in practice, it has come at an enormous environmental cost. Geographically, the majority of Iran's land is deemed to have "unsuitable" or "very poor" soil, terrain, and precipitation for agriculture. Farming in these land categories is considered to be water-intensive, conducive to land degradation, and as much as 5.5 times more inefficient than farming in a "medium" suitability class. Yet based on the current allocation of farmland and the relatively low composition of fertile land in Iran overall, a "sizable acreage" currently occurs on land "unsuitable" or "very poor" for farming.[394] In Iran, the agriculture

---

392 Bodetti, "Iran Struggles With Food."

393 Ibid.

394 Mohsen B. Mesgaran et al., "Iran's Land Suitability for Agriculture," *Scientific Reports* 7, no. 1 (August 9, 2017): 7670.

industry uses over 90 percent of the country's entire water supply.[395] Thus, the country's food and agricultural policies, designed to counteract sanctions and international isolation, is highly incompatible with the country's geography.

Although much of the environmental stress is also due to rapid population growth and poor policy choices that misallocate resources in a country where water and fertile land is naturally scarce, sanctions have impeded the transfer of knowledge and technology that would reduce the agricultural reliance on water. According to a 2017 report by the Danish Agriculture and Food Council, farming machinery in Iran "are in many cases worn out, many farms have not implemented mechanization and Iranian farmers are in most cases using antiquated farming techniques."[396] Because sanctions have restricted Iran's access to new information and technology, "both the agricultural sector and the area of food production has suffered."[397] Relative to the EU, Iran's degree of agricultural mechanization is approximately five-fold lower. Because of these outdated practices and old machinery, Iran produces much lower crop yields than would otherwise be possible. In other words, the same quantity of goods requires more land and water in Iran than in countries with more updated farming techniques.[398] For instance, it takes about twice as much water to produce the same amount of wheat in Iran as in other parts of the world.[399] Yet, access to knowledge

395 Thomas Erdbrink, "Scarred Riverbeds and Dead Pistachio Trees in a Parched Iran," *The New York Times*, December 18, 2015, sec. World.

396 The Royal Danish Embassy in Tehran, "The Agriculture and Food Market in Iran" (Danish Agriculture & Food Council, March 2017), 12.

397 Ibid, 4.

398 "Iran Water Industry Counting the Cost of US Sanctions," Eghtesad Online, October 6, 2019.

399 UNDP, "Hamoun Wetlands."

and technology that could relieve the strain on Iran's water supply has been restricted as a consequence of sanctions.

Local companies that facilitate water infrastructure modernization have experienced difficulties importing equipment, parts, and raw materials.[400] Everything from modern irrigation systems, water transfer pipes, and control units, to systems for collecting and recycling wastewater is "highly required" to increase water efficiency in Iran, but is obstructed by secondary sanctions.[401]

At the 2019 International Water and Wastewater Exhibition, the sales manager for an Iranian distributor of a Taiwanese water filter manufacturing company, Nafiseh Haghighat Javan, spoke about issues facing her business. "Fluctuations in the currency market and sanctions have created many problems regarding cooperation with Easywell to the point that we decided to turn to domestic production," she said, acknowledging the financial and political risks that Taiwan faces if the country continues to export under the secondary sanctions. The ten-year collaboration between Easywell and its Iranian counterpart has been forced into a hiatus as exporting from Taiwan "is not possible at the moment."[402]

Despite needing to reduce foreign dependence, Iran "so far does not have the technology" to achieve self-sufficiency in the industry. "Truth be said, no local manufacturer can claim he/she makes all the equipment and devices inside the country," said Javan.[403] As in the cases of other goods, high-quality water treatment products "are either not accessible" or too expensive. For raw materials inside filters,

---

400 Erdbrink, "Scarred Riverbeds."
401 Royal Danish Embassy, "Agriculture and Food Market."
402 Eghtesad Online, "Iran Water Industry."
403 Ibid.

domestic products "regrettably... do not meet the global standards." Another sales manager that imports German and Japanese products that ensure the quality of treated wastewater spoke similarly of how sanctions impeded his business. He stated, "We cannot buy electrical parts from the US or Japan and have access only to Chinese parts. Honestly speaking, the final product is not as accurate as it should be. However, the price is more competitive."[404]

International organizations such as the World Bank have also struggled to help improve Iran's water problem. In a 2014 audit evaluating the effectiveness of World Bank projects that were aimed to reform Iran's water management practices, sanctions were cited six times as the reason for unsatisfactory outcomes.[405] The report stated, "By far the largest issue was the sanctions on trade, international flow of funds and banking that Iran experienced from the third year of the project, although at time of appraisal, the broad scope of the eventual sanctions could not be foreseen."[406] Other sanctions-related issues include "procurement disruptions" and problems with the transfer of funds through intermediary banks.[407] Interestingly, the government demonstrated its commitment by allocating $50 million to the project to sustain funding even when banking and trade sanctions had threatened project financing.[408] According to the Atlantic Council in 2019, the World Bank's Iran Page had issued a disclaimer stating that

---

404 Ibid.

405 Mana Mostatabi, "Sanctioning Iran's Climate," *Atlantic Council* (blog), May 1, 2019.

406 ICR Independent Evaluation Group, "IEG: ICR Review" (World Bank Group, April 29, 2014).

407 Ibid.

408 Ibid.

the bank, in compliance with sanctions, "has not approved any new lending to Iran since 2005."[409]

With the domestic resources and infrastructures available, Iran has had to rely on poorly built dams and reservoirs, rainfall, or illegal wells for irrigation. Many of the existing dams are not operating at full capacity due to insufficient rain.[410] While the government has used cloud seeding—adding chemicals to the air to artificially increase precipitation—the environmental consequences of this procedure are unclear, and it is doubtful that the approach would have any lasting consequences to Iran's drought problem.[411, 412] Low water supply and high demand have resulted in farmers obtaining water through illegal means, such as digging wells or installing pumps to extract water.[413]

Given Iran's dire environmental and economic outlook, farmers look to short-term gains from "stealing" as much water as they can and "selling up" as it runs out.[414] However, these illegal wells often come from sources that the government has tried to set aside for sustainability purposes, and many have come up dry even below 600 feet.[415, 416] There have also been desalination efforts, but pumping desalinated water to higher altitudes is energy-intensive—so much so that transporting enough water for farmers in central Iran

---

409 Mostatabi, "Sanctioning Iran's Climate."
410 Tamer Badawi, "Iran's Water Problem," Carnegie Endowment for International Peace, December 11, 2018.
411 Ibid.
412 Jessica Brown, "Cloud Seeding: Should We Be Playing God and Controlling the Weather?," *The Independent*, January 17, 2018.
413 Badawi, "Iran's Water Problem."
414 Lewis and Madani, "End of Sanctions."
415 Badawi, "Iran's Water Problem."
416 Erdbrink, "Scarred Riverbeds."

to grow 10 percent of its wheat would take up 10 percent of the entire country's natural gas consumption.[417] According to Mori during our conversation, the desalination technology that continues to function on some of Iran's southern Islands was acquired from Israel prior to the 1979 revolution.

From the combination of legal and illegal water extraction, Iran uses as much as 3.8 billion cubic meters of water more than can be replenished and has one of the fastest groundwater depletion rates in the world.[418, 419] Those who drink water from wells often find it contaminated by salt and other residues, and many have developed kidney stones as a result. Amin, whose family owns a dried-up pistachio grove in southern Iran, said, "The irony is... that I have to drink even more water to reduce the pain."[420]

The JCPOA provided a glimmer of hope for Iran's water crisis. In the wake of eased sanctions, the Iranian government "quickly moved to attract investment and technical collaboration in its water infrastructure, utilities, and agricultural sectors," and foreign nations such as Denmark, Germany, Sweden, France, and Italy offered their support.[421, 422, 423]

While lifting sanctions would not "automatically reverse" the environmental situation in Iran, access to foreign direct investment, technology, and expertise would have a

417 Badawi, "Iran's Water Problem."
418 Bozorgmehr Sharafedin, "Iran's Thirsty Energy Industry Runs up against Water Shortage," *Reuters*, October 29, 2019.
419 Somini Sengupta, "Warming, Water Crisis, Then Unrest: How Iran Fits an Alarming Pattern," *The New York Times*, January 18, 2018, sec. Climate.
420 Erdbrink, "Scarred Riverbeds."
421 Lewis and Madani, "End of Sanctions."
422 Lyse Doucet, "Nuclear Deal Could Give Iran Technologies to Cut Pollution," *BBC News*, November 30, 2015, sec. Asia.
423 David Michel, "Iran's Impending Water Crisis," 2017.

replenishing effect in the long run for Iran's "ailing indus-tries." Moreover, stimulating the Iranian economy would free up government funds to combat the water crisis and other national priorities.[424]

However, these aspirations have been short-lived. "The doubling down of the Trump administration on the question of regime change in Iran, combined with the re-introduction of punitive sanctions against Iran, dramatically diminishes the prospects for any serious water reform in Iran," wrote Connor Dilleen for the Australian Strategic Policy Institute, "The re-imposition of broad-based sanctions will also likely limit Iran's ability to leverage external technical expertise and technologies relevant to best practice in water conser-vation, and potentially even its capacity to meet a growing shortfall in food supply."[425]

Biodiversity Loss

Wildlife survival is also at stake. According to the Depart-ment of Environment, of the 1,200 species of animals in Iran, about 15 to 20 percent are "threatened with extinction." Moreover, around twelve to sixty animals in the country are "critically endangered" as of 2019.[426] For the Asiatic chee-tah—which can now only be found in Iran—about fifty are

---

424 Aryn Baker, "A Side Effect of Iranian Sanctions: Tehran's Bad Air," *Time*, July 7, 2014.

425 Dilleen, "Will Renewed US Sanction."

426 "150 Animals in Danger of Extinction in Iran," Tehran Times, April 13, 2019.

estimated to be remaining in the world. Approximately 165 types of plants in Iran are also threatened.[427]

Shirin Hakim, a PhD scholar studying the environmental impacts of sanctions wrote, "When a country is battling sanctions, often bare necessities such as the supply of food, medical care and sustaining the local economy become priorities, and issues such as the environment lose significance." She noted that these more pressing domestic issues have led to the decline of the government's environmental budget: "Operating with fewer economic resources makes it increasingly difficult for the government to not only hire, but also provide employees with necessary equipment and monitoring technologies to preserve biodiversity."[428]

Not only have sanctions indirectly affected the government's environmental protection capacity, but they have also directly thwarted the conservation process. The Global Environmental Facility (GEF), a World Bank subsidiary, had granted Iran $7.6 million towards multiyear projects to protect biodiversity—but funds were blocked by US sanctions in 2014.[429] Travel barriers and other sanctions-related problems also likely prevent the exchange of information between foreign conservation experts and those living in Iran. The Society for Worldwide Interbank Financial Telecommunications (SWIFT), which processes funds electronically and is used for most international transfers, disconnected Iranian banks from the system in 2018. Local scientists have consequently struggled

427 Walker, "Hitting Nature Where It Hurts: Iran Feels the Pernicious Effects of US Sanctions on Biodiversity Conservation," Equal Times, February 27, 2019.

428 Syed Zafar Mehdi, "US Sanctions Cause Environmental Crisis in Iran," Anadolu Agency (AA), December 20, 2019.

429 Mehdi, "US Sanctions."

to purchase basic equipment to monitor wildlife—an essential step in the conservation process, having to instead rely on volunteer passengers to carry camera equipment or radio tracking collars into the country.[430, 431] As eight wrote in a letter to the academic journal, *Science*, "Sanctions reduce opportunities to transfer international expertise and skills and erect barriers to international financial support, which together limit the capacity of conservationists within sanctioned countries to enact effective conservation interventions."[432]

Oil

Beyond water and wildlife-related environmental issues in Iran, a direct effect of US sanctions has been the domestic usage of oil by-products and production of gasoline. "Sanctions significantly contributed to pollution, and particularly the kinds of pollution that are damaging to health," said economist and sanctions expert, Rocky Ansari.[433] While Iran has one of the world's largest proven petroleum reserves, it typically exported most of its petroleum and depended on imports for more refined fuel types such as gasoline.[434] However, the recent decade of sanctions has explicitly restricted gasoline imports—as well as equipment or services that "would help Iran make or import gasoline."[435] In order to

430   Walker, "Hitting Nature Where It Hurts."
431   Erdbrink, "Video: The Empty River of Life."
432   L. Khalatbari et al., "Sanctioning to Extinction in Iran," *Science* 362, no. 6420 (December 14, 2018): 1255-1255.
433   Baker, "A Side Effect."
434   Ibid.
435   Katzman, "Iran Sanctions."

supply its cars, trucks, and motorcycles with fuel, Iran has resorted to transforming its petrochemical plants—which usually produce plastics—into refineries.[436, 437] This "expensive and inefficient process" produces low-quality gasoline "choked with pollutants."[438]

In addition to the issue of oil refineries themselves, there is also the issue of what they produce. To increase the domestic supply of gasoline, benzenes, and methyl tertiary-butyl ether (MTBE) are added into the mix—additives that are banned in most Western countries due to health concerns.[439]

Moreover, one of the by-products of Iran's relatively primitive oil refineries is mazut, a "low quality fuel oil with an obnoxious smell." In the US and Europe, this viscous, black substance can be further processed into diesel. Yet in Iran, the refineries—most of which were built during the pre-revolutionary era—not only lack the capacity to break down this material, but also produce a higher ratio of mazut relative to more modern processes. Using these antiquated refineries, around 24 percent of crude oil is turned into mazut. "The level of sulfur density in mazut produced in Iran is nearly 3.5 percent, which is seven times more than the international standard for vessels on high seas, and its usage is strictly banned in urban areas, specifically in the cities like Tehran that are struggling with air pollution," reported Radio Farda on the toxicity of this substance.[440]

436 Mostatabi, "Sanctioning Iran's Climate."
437 Vida Balikhani, "Poor Quality Gasoline Deadly for Iranians," *Atlantic Council* (blog), February 16, 2017.
438 Baker, "A Side Effect."
439 Balikhani, "Poor Quality Gasoline."
440 "Harmful Oil Bi-Product Used In Iranian Cities, Polluting The Air," Radio Farda, January 19, 2020.

Thus, unfortunately because of oil sanctions, major environmental problems are created in Iran. Not only does the usage of old petrochemical factories to refine oil cause dangerous air pollution, but the country has also been barred from exporting mazut—meaning that Iran has no choice but to burn the substance domestically in its electricity plants. According to Isa Kalantari, the Department of Environment chief, regretfully, "Iran is caught in a vicious circle of air pollution, without knowing how to find a way out." In under a year, by January 2020, nearly 99 million cubic feet of mazut had been fed to Iranian power plants. "Having clean air has become an impossible dream for Iranians," he said.[441]

When sanctions were temporarily lifted, the change in visibility was dramatic. "Now that hardly any petrol from petrochemical factories is being used, the pollution has reduced, and already people can breathe better air," said Ansari during this period of environmental relief. The snow mountains surrounding the capital city were once again visible.[442]

Companies like Daelim Industrial Company and Hyundai Engineering from South Korea agreed in late 2016 to early 2017 to help various Iranian oil refining companies to update their oil refineries, with each deal worth billions of US dollars.[443] Yet by 2018 when sanctions were reimposed, both projects were canceled.[444, 445]

441 Ibid.
442 Baker, "A Side Effect."
443 "Daelim Revokes W2tln Deal with Iranian Oil Company in Wake," The Korea Herald, June 1, 2018.
444 Ibid.
445 Reuters Staff, "South Korea's Hyundai E&C Cancels $521 Million Petrochemicals Deal, Cites Iran Financing Failure," Reuters, October 29, 2018.

Iran's Environmental Future

Iran, as evidenced by the Supreme Leader's directives, is aware of and aims to mitigate climate change as well as environmental issues such as desertification, pollution, and drought. In a speech just before the 2015 Paris Climate Change Conference (COP 21), Khamenei stressed the importance of expanding a "green economy" that increased dependence on renewable energy sources and improved waste management. Moreover, Khamenei supported increasing "environmental diplomacy" and "bilateral, multilateral, regional and international partnerships and targeted cooperation in the environmental field."[446]

At the Paris Climate Conference in 2015, Iran pledged to reduce emissions by 12 percent, devote $5 billion towards conservation, and cut greenhouse gas emissions by 4 percent so long as sanctions were not reimposed.[447] The country remained committed to environmental issues in 2017—when it proposed to add the water-related issues to the agenda of the next Climate Conference (COP 24). Kaveh Madani, deputy head of the Department of Environment on Research and Education at the COP 23 conference, said "Four decades of international and extraterritorial sanctions have had a multiplier effect on the adverse impacts of climate change on Iran, resulting in environmental degradation. The imposition of unilateral coercive economic measures contrary to the international law by some developed countries [...] decrease the

---

446 Arash Karami, "Khamenei Says Iran Must Go Green," Al-Monitor, November 18, 2015.

447 Mostatabi, "Sanctioning Iran's Climate."

countries' ability to cope with the adverse impacts of climate change and violate the rights of many people."[448]

During the period of sanctions relief, a "flurry" of foreign interest presented itself to Iran. Based on the country's natural landscape, half of its domestic energy needs can be satisfied by solar and wind energy.[449] Renewable energy companies like the UK's Quercus, Germany's Siemens, and Norway's Saga Energy initiated multimillion-dollar projects with Iran.[450, 451] As a report on behalf of the German Environment Agency recalls about this period, "within two months of JCPOA signing, four contracts for solar projects were signed for approximately 1,150 MW (for context, Iran's solar capacity grew from 53 MW in 2005 to 67 MW by 2011). Furthermore, Danish multinational Vestas committed to investing $100 million in Iranian wind infrastructure, and a German venture pledged to develop a 48 MW wind farm. Finally, $75 million investment was pledged for developing a waste-to-energy plant."[452]

But once again, when the sanctions snapback occurred, Quercus announced its decision to "cease all activities" in Iran, including its $570 million plan to construct a solar power plant. Siemens refused to accept new orders from Iran, and Saga Energy's solar energy construction project was delayed due to difficulties in receiving funding.[453, 454]

---

448 "Iran Proposes Inclusion of Water-Related Issues in COP 24," Tehran Times, November 22, 2017.

449 Mostatabi, "Sanctioning Iran's Climate."

450 Ibid.

451 María Yetano Roche, Cordelia Paetz, and Carmen Dienst, "Implementation of Nationally Determined Contributions—Islamic Republic of Iran," Umwelt Bundesamt, 2018, 42.

452 Ibid, 38.

453 Mostatabi, "Sanctioning Iran's Climate."

454 Roche, Paetz, and Dienst, "Implementation."

***

Sanctions imposed on Iran are supposed to reduce its chances of acquiring a nuclear weapon, curb its regional activities, and condemn human rights abuses. But what has happened as a result is an environmental disaster, which not only directly affects the human rights of Iranian people but also has devastating and long-term consequences to the entire global population. Disease from polluted air, forced migration due to poor environmental conditions and water scarcity, and food insecurity are only some of the problems facing Iranian people today. The toxic chemicals from its domestic oil refineries are released into the atmosphere—which is shared by Americans and Iranians alike. Preventing Iran from updating its energy production systems is, in the long-run, detrimental to everyone's ability to enjoy clean air. The Communication Director at the National Iranian American Council (NIAC) writes, "To support the Iranian people means empowering those dedicated to stewarding Iran's resources—not weaponizing access to food, land, and water."[455]

---

455 Mostatabi, "Sanctioning Iran's Climate."

CHAPTER 7

HOUSING

Owning a house is considered to be an important status symbol in Iran.[456] Often, it is the only thing that middle-class families leave for their children as an inheritance.[457] The importance of a home in Persian culture is exemplified by the popular proverb "*čahār divāri, ektiāri*," which roughly translates to "four walls, own discretion," or "one is master in one's own house."[458]

Partially due to urbanization and better employment opportunities in cities, the urban population has increased dramatically since the late twentieth century.[459] To accommodate the increasing population, houses with secluded gardens, courtyards, or big terraces that had been "cornerstones"

---

456 Habibollah Zanjani, "Housing in Iran," Encyclopaedia Iranica, March 23, 2012.

457 Monavar Khalaj, "Sanction End to Help Iran Property Market," *Financial Times*, September 15, 2015.

458 Zanjani, "Housing in Iran."

459 Zohreh Fanni, "Cities and Urbanization in Iran after the Islamic Revolution," *Cities* 23 (December 1, 2006): 407-11.

of Iranian architecture gave way to apartment buildings.[460] Although official statistics suggest that approximately two out of three Iranians were homeowners as of 2015, the reality of high prices and insufficient wages suggests a very different picture.[461]

The 2011-2012 sanctions period exacerbated Iran's housing bubble. Wealthy Iranians who could not move their money out of the country or wanted a stable asset during uncertain economic conditions invested in real estate.[462] On the other hand, rapid inflation, free-falling currency, and rising unemployment made housing increasingly expensive to ordinary Iranians.[463] By 2013, real-estate prices of luxury apartments had tripled within two years.[464]

Housing became a major stressor for many people, who would see deposit prices for rental apartments increase by the month. On average, these deposits would cost around $6,000, in a country where the average worker's salary was less than $200 a month. "Things get pretty desperate," said Ali, a twenty-eight-year-old art teacher. "What do you expect from an ordinary teacher who makes [$250] a month?"[465]

Reza, a sixty-year-old pensioner, had been hoping to receive additional income from renting out his one-bedroom flat in Tehran. He had drawn up a two-year contract with

---

460 Salman Parviz, "Despite Economic Fallout Tehran Real Estate Market Flourishes," Tehran Times, June 30, 2020.

461 Khalaj, "Sanction End."

462 "Fear of Bubble as Sanctions Stoke Iran Property Boom," VOA News, May 8, 2013.

463 Tehran Bureau correspondent, "Tehran Landlords and Tenants Lock Horns in Heat of Property Boom," The Guardian, February 5, 2013, sec. World news.

464 VOA News, "Fear of Bubble."

465 Tehran Bureau correspondent, "Tehran Landlords."

his tenants, but the worsening economy from the 2012-2013 sanctions devalued this source of income by more than half, while his living expenses were increasing twofold. He could not sell the home to pay for his expenses—his tenants refused to leave as it was the best deal they could obtain. "For a person like me at this age, the most important thing is living in peace, but imagine not having enough money to fix the car to go to the doctor. I've no idea what's going to happen, but I worry," he said.[466]

When the US withdrew from the JCPOA and reimposed sanctions in 2018, Iran's housing crisis deepened. Similar to the previous period, Iranians' decreasing purchasing power, high import costs for construction material, and the use of properties as investments for the rich once again resulted in exorbitant housing prices. As the majority of Iranians can no longer afford to buy a house, tens of thousands of apartments lie empty in new towns.[467] Other apartments are purchased but vacant because property owners are unwilling to lease their luxury apartments at lower prices.[468] As many as 490,000 homes in or near Tehran are estimated to be empty—with 40,000 of the vacancies occurring within the past year.[469] Throughout the country, while 26.6 million Iranians live in "rented squalid homes and apartments," 2.5 million homes are uninhabited as of 2019.[470]

---

466 Ibid.

467 Robin Wright, "Ghost Towers: The View from Iran's Housing Crisis," *The New Yorker*, accessed October 22, 2020.

468 Adele Nima, "26 Million Denied Homes as Iran's Housing Market Prices Jump by 90%," *Iran News Wire* (blog), June 25, 2019.

469 Karin Laub and Mohammad Nasiri, "US Sanctions Squeeze Iran Middle Class, Upend Housing Sector," AP News, July 23, 2019.

470 Nima, "26 Million Denied Homes."

For those with the capacity to invest, housing has become a site for "get-rich-quick schemes". According to the former Chief Economist of Ashland Oil, Cyrus Tahmassebi, "Buyers flip it [sell a property] within six months or so for a big profit and the new buyer would do the same only a few months later."[471] From 2018 to 2020, the price for the smallest-sized apartments in Tehran had tripled from 70 million rials to 190 million rials. According to the International Institute for Iranian Studies, it would take a young working couple twelve years to purchase a 40 square-meter (430 square-foot) apartment, assuming they save all the money they earn, and prices remain stable.[472]

Those who rent may spend as much as 80 percent of their monthly salaries on housing, if not more.[473] Others have had no choice but to leave proper housing. The number of people living in slums and shanty-towns doubled within two years, from 19 million in 2018 to 38 million in 2020.[474]

The price of land in some parts of Tehran has become three times more expensive within seven months, Mori said in October 2020. He predicted, "I don't think it's going to drop down. Things are out of control… it's not in their hands anymore."

Given the volatile economic conditions where prices and employment status are in flux, a person's ability to buy a house also changes regularly. Koohyar reflected to me, "[I]

---

471 Tehran Bureau correspondent, "Tehran Landlords."

472 Rasanah Editorial Team, "25 Square Meter Apartments: The Contradiction between Iran's New Housing Policy and Its Official Population Policy," *Rasanah International Institute for Iranian Studies* (blog), August 5, 2020.

473 Jubin Katiraie, "The Nightmare of Rising Prices and Housing Rent in Iran," *Iran Focus* (blog), June 22, 2020.

474 Rasanah Editorial Team, "25 Square Meter Apartments."

cannot plan because now maybe I can afford a house, but tomorrow I don't know if I'll still have a job."

Even for those who are brave enough to commit, the unexpected price fluctuations give them no choice but to make new arrangements. "Before the prices went up, I could have purchased a 100-meter apartment around Jomhouri Square [the central Tehran area] if my loan was approved earlier," said Mehrdad, a forty-year-old Tehran local in 2019. He had been saving up for years to buy an apartment for his family. "Now I can't even afford a seventy-meter apartment in the southern parts of the town, where the prices are lower."[475]

For others, homeownership is no longer a reality—unless they made the purchase prior to the harsh sanctions. "You either have a house from before or you'll never be able to buy a house. Now it's impossible; they're too expensive," A, a tour guide in Isfahan, stated in our conversation. As a small business owner, M echoed his sentiment: "Buying houses is almost impossible for the majority of the people." According to the International Institute for Iranian Studies, a young working couple would need to save for twelve years to afford a forty square meter apartment using 2020 prices, without accounting for food or other living expenses.[476]

Those who have worked hard to move into better neighborhoods are being priced out. Maryam Alidadi, a stay-at-home-mom who formerly worked as a government employee and her husband, a mechanic, used to rent a "spacious" apartment in Tehran's city center. They had enough disposable income to own a car, go on vacations, and eat out at restaurants on occasion. Since the "fallout" from US

475 Maysam Bizaer, "Iranians Struggle to Afford Housing as Prices Soar," Al Jazeera, August 5, 2019.
476 Rasanah Editorial Team, "25 Square Meter Apartments."

sanctions, they have had to move to an eighty-two-square-meter (880 sq ft) apartment on the outskirts of Tehran, selling their car and borrowing from friends to make ends meet. "Our standard of living has dropped considerably," said Maryam.[477]

The Alidadis are not the only ones to move. The *Financial Times* interviewed other impacted locals. "I hate living here but have no other choice. I feel so down whenever I go to Tehran, the city where I was born and grew up," said Farzaneh. Unable to afford the rent increase, Farzaneh's family had relocated to Parand, "a dusty satellite town" south-west of the capital. As a mother of a six-year-old daughter, she worried about the area's social problems. Unemployment, in combination with the lack of recreational facilities, contributed to boredom and risk-taking behavior. "Young men find refuge in drugs, violence and sitting idly out in the streets," said the owner of a grocery store. "I guess no one leaves Tehran to live or work here unless they feel miserable like me," said another man named Arash, the owner of a tea house in Parand.[478]

Mori's way of remaining in Tehran is to live and work in a hostel. Based on what was available, it seemed like the best option for him. After what he calls the "crazy experience" with his family business in interior design, he wanted to work somewhere where he "didn't have to invest any money." According to Mori, the hostel is the biggest in the country and best-located in the capital. 80 percent of all young travelers who were in Iran had stayed at the hostel at some point during their trip.

---

477 Laub and Mohammad Nasiri, "US Sanctions."

478 Monavar Khalaj, "Impoverished Iranians Forced to Leave Tehran for a Cheaper Life," *Financial Times*, September 29, 2019.

Even during the coronavirus pandemic, the hostel managed to stay open by allowing domestic travelers. Nevertheless, housing costs have swallowed an outsized proportion of his income. "[The hostel's] full but we are not earning money," he said. "Every year, we have to pay an extra thirty percent for rent."

Recognizing the housing crisis, the government has throughout the years attempted to improve the living conditions for the middle- and working-class. In the last decade, President Ahmadinejad launched the Mehr Housing Project, which was supposed to create affordable housing units for low-income families through cheap, ninety-nine-year mortgages.[479] But due to a myriad of reasons including corruption, poor planning, and increased construction costs, the project is largely seen as a massive failure.[480] Not only did it supply the public with significantly fewer units than had been promised, but it also created a "new category of housing" that made the affordable housing unaffordable to even the "relatively well-off," as racketeers frequently used complicit applicants as intermediaries to purchase these cheap apartments and sell them at much higher prices.[481] The Mehr Housing Project also absorbed many of the loan facilities that otherwise could have been provided to middle-class families as mortgages or for house construction.[482]

Under President Rouhani, the "National Housing Initiative" was launched in 2019 as a renewed attempt to meet some

479 Marketa Hulpachova, "Iran's Economy Struggles to Support Ahmadinejad's Ill-Conceived Housing Vision," *The Guardian*, January 30, 2014, sec. World news.

480 Bijan Khajehpour, "Iran's Housing Crisis," Al-Monitor, June 17, 2013.

481 Hulpachova, "Iran's Economy Struggles."

482 Khajehpour, "Iran's Housing Crisis."

of the demands for affordable housing.[483] Yet, many remain skeptical of these new projects, as they fail to address the root of the problem. "The problem is not with these [government] plans," said Mehrdad, the local whose delayed loan approval caused him to lose the 100-meter apartment. "The main issue is the gap [now] between our wage and the actual inflation, which is growing bigger and bigger every year."[484]

***

Sanctions have compounded the effects of poor government policies and corruption. As illustrated by the real estate market, there is growing inequality between the wealthy elites and everyone else. Whereas everyone has the right to an adequate standard of living—including housing—according to the Universal Declaration of Human Rights, the standard of living for ordinary Iranian people has been deteriorating. Decent housing is increasingly unattainable.

In order to reduce speculation, Iran needs to regain the balance between supply and demand in the housing market, ideally alongside a "healthy and balanced economic growth"—which could help restore people's purchasing power.[485] However, the readjustment of the country's housing sector requires long-term stability. Even if sanctions were to be lifted, a lot of uncertainties would remain. Alongside economic improvement, a cohesive public policy would also be necessary to improve the housing conditions of many Iranian people.

---

483 "1st Phase of National Housing Action Plan Completed in Southern Iran," *Tehran Times*, May 30, 2020.

484 Bizaer, "Iranians Struggle."

485 Khajehpour, "Iran's Housing Crisis."

CHAPTER 8

EDUCATION

———

"I should say that the education system in Iran is not the way people might imagine here. As a graduate student at Harvard, I had to explain quite a few times that I was allowed to attend a university as a woman in Iran. While it is true that boys and girls go to separate schools up to high school, this does not prevent them from participating, say, in the Olympiads or the summer camps."

—MARYAM MIRZAKHANI[486]

Maryam Mirzakhani was the first woman to win the Fields Medal, the most prestigious prize in mathematics. She was also the first woman to compete on the Iranian math Olympiad team and the first to achieve a perfect score. While her success as a mathematician can in a large part be attributed to her personal talents, she also credited attending good

---

486 Guardian Staff, "Maryam Mirzakhani: 'The More I Spent Time on Maths, the More Excited I Got,'" *The Guardian*, August 13, 2014, sec. Science.

schools and having good teachers and mentors.[487] As a young girl, she had not been "interested in thinking about" math. It was her older brother who introduced her to mathematical concepts and her high school teacher who challenged her in advanced mathematics and who, among others, helped her see the beauty in math.[488, 489]

Perhaps due to its history as a pioneer in every field from architecture, art, and literature to science, technology, and engineering, Iran has a strong cultural emphasis on education. Relative to other countries in the region, Iran is a "very educated society"—its metrics consistently outperforming regional statistics.[490] For instance, its net primary school enrollment rate was 99.7 percent as of 2017, whereas the average rate for the Middle East and North Africa (MENA) was at 93.5 percent.[491] Similarly, the 2017 net enrollment rate for secondary education was 81.4 percent relative to 72.4 percent in the region.[492] According to a 2015 article, parents take their adolescent's preparation for the university entrance exam ("Konkur") so seriously that the term "Konkur quarantine" has become a common term, referring to the entire family's devotion to the child's preparation that they forgo family vacations or social engagements.[493]

487 CBC Radio, "A Legacy of Firsts: How an Iranian Mathematician Transcended Boundaries," CBC, September 23, 2019.

488 Ibid.

489 Guardian Staff, "Maryam Mirzakhani."

490 CBC Radio, "A Legacy of Firsts."

491 "School Enrollment, Primary (% Net)—Middle East & North Africa, Iran, Islamic Rep.," World Bank, accessed October 23, 2020.

492 "School Enrollment, Secondary (% Net)—Middle East & North Africa, Iran, Islamic Rep.," World Bank.

493 Samira Hazari, "What does school look like in Iran?" British Council, 21 April 2015.

Iran's central government exerts "strong control" over the national education system. With this authority, it had reversed much of the pro-western practices that had existed under the Shah prior to the revolution.[494] As a consequence of the "Islamization of school" under the Islamic Republic, Iran has adopted a pedagogy that teaches "*from* religion" rather than "*about* religion."[495] Schools are separated by sex, and in higher education students' successes are dependent on their "adherence to prevalent political dogma" and "personal piety, either real or perceived."[496] Nevertheless, in many aspects they are similar to those in other countries—along with more religious studies, subjects such as math, science, social sciences, literature, and art are taught; students also take field trips to museums or the cinema, and have to do sports.[497]

Maybe in part recognizing the value of education as a tool for promoting its religious and political ideology, the government has made major efforts to increase literacy. Primary and secondary education is free in Iran, school is compulsory until ninth grade, and the university attendance rate is targeted to be at 60 percent by 2025—which, as of 2015, it was "well on pace" to reach.[498, 499] Private primary education also exists, as well as "Nemuneh Mardomi" schools—highly competitive, partially public schools that provide quality education at a more affordable price.[500]

494 WES Staff, "Education in Iran," World Education News + Reviews (WENR), February 7, 2017.
495 World Bank, "School Enrollment, Secondary."
496 "Iran—Education," Encyclopedia Britannica, accessed October 23, 2020.
497 "Iran's Literacy Rate up to 97%," Tehran Times, September 23, 2018.
498 Hamid Mojtahedi, "Investing in Iran's Education Sector," Al Tamimi & Co, published August 2016.
499 WES Staff, "Education in Iran."
500 Tehran Times, "Iran's Literacy Rate."

Much of the continued rise in literacy rates (98.2 percent for those between 10-49 years of age) can also be attributed to the increased education of girls in recent decades.[501] Whereas more than 60 percent of women were illiterate in the late twentieth century, by 2015 the female literacy rate had reached about 80 percent, and more women than men had been enrolling in universities.[502, 503] In 2018, Iran's Literacy Movement Organization (headed by the Vice-Minister of Education) was awarded the UNESCO Confucius Prize for Literacy based on its program that promotes literacy and computer skills, focusing particularly on "women and girls in rural areas, minorities, factory workers, and people in detention."[504]

In 2015, educational coverage was extended to refugees and non-Iranian citizens. Iran's Supreme Leader Ayatollah Khamenei decreed that all foreign nationals are allowed to attend schools: "No Afghan child, not even immigrants who came to Iran illegally and without documents, must be kept from an education and all of them must be registered in Iranian schools."[505, 506]

Since the late twentieth century, interstate and civil wars, as well as Taliban control of Afghanistan have resulted in a significant Afghan population in Iran. Though Afghan refugees still

501 "Literacy Movement Organization Drafts Proposal on Compulsory Education," Tehran Times, October 6, 2018.

502 "Iran (Islamic Republic Of)," UNESCO Institute of Statics, November 27, 2016.

503 Zahra Mila Elmi, "Educational Attainment in Iran," Middle East Institute, January 29, 2009, accessed October 22, 2020.

504 The Islamic Republic News Agency, "Iran's literacy movement wins UNESCO Confucius Prize," Islamic Republic News Agency, September 9, 2018.

505 Tehran Times, "Iran's Literacy Rate."

506 Frud Bezhan, "Class Act: Iranian Campaign to Allow Afghan Refugee Kids Into School," Radio Free Europe / Radio Liberty, September 02, 2017.

face many problems in Iran, such as the risk of deportation, Iran "leads by example" relative to other countries in its inclusion of refugees in publicly-provided services, and the conditions for this vulnerable population has been improving.[507, 508]

The UN High Commission for Refugees (UNHCR) interviewed a few such students. "I love school so much," said Parisa, one of the undocumented Afghan refugees studying at a girl's school in Isfahan, Iran. She was eleven when she first set foot in a classroom. "My favourite subject is maths, because maths is everywhere in the world. I love multiplication and division—they are really easy." When asked about her future aspirations, Parisa said she would be "very happy" to become a teacher back in Afghanistan, because children in her hometown "can't really study much." Being allowed to attend school has not only helped her discover an interest in math, but it has also changed others' perceptions of her: "I'm so happy that I can study side by side with Iranian students. People no longer say, 'Oh, you're an Afghan.'"[509]

By 2019, 480,000 Afghan children were being educated in Iranian schools—including Parisa. Of these, 130,000 of them were undocumented, and 60,000 new children had been brought into the education system in 2019 alone.[510] "No students should be forced to drop out of school," the Deputy Director for International Affairs at the Ministry of Education had said, emphasizing that tuition should not be an obstruction to Afghan children's attainment of education.[511]

507 Farha Bhoyroo, "Afghan children learn side by side with Iranian peers," *UNHCR, The UN Refugee Agency*, 10 December 2019.
508 Bezhan, "Class Act."
509 Bhoyroo, "Afghan children learn."
510 Ibid.
511 Tehran Times, "Iran's Literacy Rate."

Yet, despite receiving free education, Parisa's situation is precarious. At fifteen, Parisa's brother had to leave school, joining his father on a construction site to provide for Parisa and her younger siblings. But despite the family's hardships, Parisa's father vowed to "do everything for [his] daughters" to receive an education—to be better equipped than himself and his wife—but because of Iran's unstable job market, "it is getting harder and harder."[512]

Inflationary spikes and economic uncertainties as a result of sanctions have significantly increased the price of school supplies.[513] Added to the skyrocketing prices of food, transportation, and rent, the issue becomes one of survival, let alone education.[514] Moreover, books, journals, and magazines are becoming more and more out of reach for the "majority of Iranians" as paper and printing costs increase and people allocate a greater proportion of their income to the purchase of essentials.[515] "Books are not affordable for most people, so people prefer to watch TV and not read books," said Majid Taleghani, a publisher and bookstore owner in Tehran.[516]

The detrimental effects that sanctions have had on education are not limited to immigrant families like Parisa's. Increased economic burdens more generally incentivize families to abandon their children's education, either to work for additional income or to marry off their daughters at an early age.[517] "More than nine percent of Iranian families have to sell

---

512 Bhoyroo, "Afghan children learn."
513 ICHRI, "A Growing Crisis".
514 Bhoyroo, "Afghan children learn."
515 ICHRI, "A Growing Crisis," 141.
516 Ramin Mostaghim and Melissa Etehad, "Middle-class Iranians resort to buying rottng produce as U.S. sanctions take toll," *Los Angeles Times,* August 28, 2019.
517 ICHRI, "A Growing Crisis," 125.

their furniture and home appliances due to the fact that they cannot pay for education with their normal income," said Mohammadreza Vaez Mahdavi, an adviser to the Minister of Cooperatives, Labor and Social Welfare.[518]

Although school enrollment rates remain relatively high, there is a significant drop-off in enrollment after primary education. In 2016, only about two-thirds of fifteen-year-olds in the poorest 20 percent of the population remained in school, and by nineteen, school enrollment among this group had dropped to about 25 percent.[519] Girls and poor children have been increasingly dropping out of the education system at all levels. According to official estimates in 2019, 53 percent of dropouts are caused by "financial difficulties." Unfortunately, many of these children are likely to become part of the 2 to 7 million total child laborers in Iran.[520]

Besides the troubles for students, economic problems pose hardships for teachers as well, which inevitably affects the quality of education for the worse. Vahid Mahmoudi, economist and university professor has stated that "69 percent of the teachers drive taxis as their second job and 54 percent of the teachers have low income and little time."[521] This sentiment is shared by the Minister of Education: "Teachers have always had to have a second job to earn their living. Without any exaggerations, if a teacher wants to earn his/her living just by teaching, they cannot have an average life."[522] The task

---

518 Arvin Khoshnood, "Poverty in Iran: A Critical Analysis," *Middle East Policy* 26, no. 1 (2019): 60-74.

519 World Bank, "Iran Economic Monitor."

520 "Repressive State and Low Quality of Education in Iran," *Iran HRM* (blog), September 22, 2019.

521 Ibid.

522 Khoshnood, "Poverty in Iran."

of providing high-quality education becomes understandably difficult if teachers, having to take two jobs, struggle to make ends meet.

Not only are the economic consequences of sanctions pushing an increasing number of Iranian people to the brink of poverty, but they have also negatively impacted the government's budget and thereby expenditure on education. In recent years, President Rouhani has had to order the closure of many schools in rural communities as a means to "cut down on budget."[523] Other schools that remain open are in conditions that desperately require renovation. For instance, as of 2017, 42 percent of Iranian schools did not have a safe heating system.[524]

Even though Iranian culture "highly esteems" literacy and the government is incentivized to improve access to education—at the very least for sociopolitical control—limited government resources and financial difficulties in many families suggests an alarming prospect for the future of education in the country. A critical way of breaking the cycle of poverty and inequality in the long run is by improving labor market conditions and managing inflation, so that people regain their purchasing power. At the same time, increasing the government budget could maintain and improve existing schooling infrastructure, particularly in rural areas. Unfortunately, the situation is unlikely to improve if sanctions and government policies continue to cripple the economy.[525]

---

523 Iran HRM, ""Repressive State."
524 Khoshnood, "Poverty in Iran."
525 World Bank, "Iran Economic Monitor."

Higher Education

Iran is home to two of the top ten largest universities in the world.[526] Students choose their majors prior to entering college and are required to pass the highly competitive "Konkur" to gain entrance to free public universities.[527, 528] STEM programs are particularly competitive. There are also private and vocational institutions such as teacher training colleges or technical programs.[529] Due to the overwhelming demand for higher education and limited capacities in existing public universities, the government has increased private or fee-based public universities since the early 2000s. As of 2015, approximately 85 percent of those enrolled in tertiary education pay out-of-pocket.[530]

From a combination of sanctions and decreased government subsidies on education, many students can no longer afford their tuition.[531] While tuition increases, inflation, declining purchasing power, and increasing poverty make tuition fees a bigger challenge for many students. "Many Iranian youths whom I have encountered privately or in the course of work have told me that they gave up their university studies because they could not pay the tuition fees, or passed the national university entrance exam several years in row, only to be admitted to a state-owned university, where the costs are lower," wrote Arvin Khoshnood in the *Middle East Policy* journal in 2019.[532]

526 WES Staff, "Education in Iran."
527 CBC Radio, "A Legacy of Firsts."
528 WES Staff, "Education in Iran."
529 Ibid.
530 Shervin Malekzadeh, "The new business of education in Iran," *Washington Post*, August 19, 2015.
531 Iran HRM, ""Repressive State."
532 Khoshnood, "Poverty in Iran."

High youth unemployment likely feeds into the negative cycle of university dropouts and youths with low purchasing power. Given the unfavorable economic conditions, Iran is "producing far more college graduates (and often of low quality) than the domestic economy can absorb." Whereby jobless students struggle to support their educational expenses, and those who drop out also struggle to find employment. About half of all unemployed youth in Iran are college-educated. Students who have graduated in the top 20 percent of their high school class and attend Tehran University, one of the most prestigious universities in Iran, have "no vision, plan, or hope for their future." The "deep frustration" amongst these ambitious young people has contributed to the socio-political instability within the country.[533]

'Brain Drain' and Other Graduate Troubles

Although in recent decades the expansion of undergraduate levels of universities through private and other fee-based institutions has provided more opportunities for youths, inadequacies persist at the graduate level. There are too few existing graduate programs for Iranian students, and the problem has contributed to the exodus of academic elites from the country—a phenomenon also known as "Brain Drain." Domestically, only 6 percent of people who applied were accepted into master's programs, while 4 percent of PhD candidates succeeded in getting a position as of 2011.[534]

---

533 Amin Mohnseni-Cheraghilou, "Update from Iran: Iran's Over-Education Crises," *World Bank Blogs* (blog), October 6, 2017.

534 WES Staff, "Education in Iran."

While the lack of academic resources may be a big factor of the "Brain Drain" phenomenon, people also look to other countries more generally for alternative sources of hope, particularly given economic and unemployment conditions. Within Iran, 20,000 PhDs were unemployed as of late 2018, with the country's mismanagement and economic difficulties compounded by sanctions.[535] "People are selling their computers, rugs, phones and jewelry to collect money" so as to leave Iran, according to a travel agent in Tehran in 2019.[536]

Over a quarter of university-educated Iranians are estimated to live and work outside of Iran. Iran thereby loses expertise and talent from hundreds of thousands of Iran's most brilliant minds, who are often trained for free in Iran. The phenomenon is so detrimental that it is estimated to cost the economy $50 billion every year.[537] With sanctions dashing hopes for a bright future in their home country, young people are increasingly desperate for better opportunities elsewhere.

Studying Abroad

Not only sanctions, but volatile US-Iran relations more broadly have posed never-ending obstacles for those determined enough to pursue their dreams of life outside of Iran. Students who have "invested [their] lives" to become the top computer engineering student at their university or to place among the top three in over 200,000 of those taking Iran's

---

535 "Twenty Thousand PhD Graduates Are Unemployed In Iran," Radio Farda, December 27, 2018.

536 Mary Jane Maxwell, "Iran's 41-Year 'Brain Drain,'" *ShareAmerica* (blog), February 4, 2020.

537 Mohnseni-Cheraghilou, "Iran's Over-Education Crises."

university entrance exam, who have been accepted to prestigious American university programs, and who have gone through the rigorous interview and visa applications processes have had their valid F-1 student visas unexpectedly revoked—with no explanation—by the American government, presumably due to the escalation of US-Iran tensions in 2019.[538]

"I thought that was the end," said S, a twenty-three-year-old student, referring to the moment she finally received her visa to the US. She had chosen to study at UC Irvine over other opportunities in Canada and Europe—with the knowledge that her visa would most probably be single-entry, and she would not be able to see her family until the end of her studies. Besides travel fees, she had paid for two months' rent, purchased furniture online for her new room, and registered to attend some scientific symposiums in anticipation of her time abroad. Her sibling, who was already in the US, had intended to pay her a surprise visit. Little did S know that within a few months, her visa would suddenly be canceled, and she would be barred from traveling to the country she had looked forward to benefiting—not to mention the personal sacrifices she had made in the process.[539]

For Iranian students like her, the financial burdens (especially given the high exchange rate) and emotional disappointment were devastating. Many had lined up work as research assistants to pay for living expenses while abroad, knowing it was their only way to afford tuition. The stress from this drastic upheaval of their life plans caused immense anxiety and deteriorated physical health. After being turned away from the

---

538 Caleb Hampton and Simon Campbell, "Iranian Students Barred from US: Lost Money, Broken Dreams, No Answers," *The Guardian*, October 14, 2019, sec. US news.

539 Ibid.

airport, S stayed in bed for days, "crying from stress for hours at a time." For the first time in her life, she started taking anxiety medication. Another disappointed student, Mehran, said, "I'm really upset and I'm really weak even in physical health." He gave up control of his award-winning software company in Tehran in order to pursue a PhD in the United States.[540]

Iranian students who were already abroad have also suffered from the secondary sanctions. Because it is difficult to send money from the US to Iran or vice versa, students in America cannot offer financial support to their families back in Iran, and parents cannot help their children with tuition or other living expenses. Although Nazanin Asadi managed to "scrape by" working multiple jobs while attending law school at the University of Southern California, she could not transfer money to help her disabled parents back in Iran. In addition to the financial stressors, there was always the "looming threat" that accidentally misreporting transactions or failing to obtain the necessary licenses would lead to US investigations. Some have actually "found the FBI at their door asking questions."[541]

Sanctions have affected students in other countries as well. More than fifty Iranian students in Norway were "ask[ed] to leave the country" in 2015 due to fear of technology transfer to Iran. One of the PhD students—who has sued Norway for her expulsion—had been studying the production of ferromanganese, a metal alloy commonly made in Iran, to make it more environmentally friendly.[542] In short, it had nothing

540 Ibid.

541 Sam Levin, "Cut off from Family, Unable to Travel: How US Sanctions Punish Iranian Americans," *The Guardian*, January 19, 2020, sec. US news.

542 Oslo Lars Bevanger, "Iranian Students Sue Norway over Expulsion," DW.COM, June 26, 2015.

to do with "sensitive technology."[543] The Norwegian University of Science and Technology (NTNU) "fully back[ed]" the Iranian students, and their program advisor agrees that their "PhD programs [were] well on the safe side of the UN and EU sanctions toward Iran."[544]

In the UK, Iranians' bank accounts were also unexpectedly closed, including for Alireza when he was a PhD student in chemical engineering. Although he was able to open a new account, the closure had "so badly hurt [his] credit history" that it has diminished his future chances of getting a mortgage.[545]

Research Barriers

For academics residing in Iran, the quality of higher education is increasingly at risk as research and exchange opportunities have been inhibited by sanctions. In particular, sanctions regimes have "increasingly denied" Iranian scholars "opportunities to publish scientific findings, attend scientific meetings," and access to "essential" laboratory supplies and other resources.[546] Clinical trials sponsored by foreign countries—such as the Wellcome Trust's study on

---

543 Saeed Kamali Dehghan, "Iranian Students Blocked from UK Stem Courses Due to US Sanctions," *The Guardian*, June 26, 2014, sec. World newsk.

544 Lars Bevanger, "Iranian Students Sue Norway."

545 Saeed Kamali Dehghan, "Iranians Sue UK Banks over Closed Accounts, Claiming Racial Discrimination," *The Guardian*, March 28, 2014, sec. World news.

546 Fatemeh Kokabisaghi et al., "Impact of United States Political Sanctions on International Collaborations and Research in Iran," *BMJ Global Health* 4, no. 5 (September 3, 2019).

reducing urban health inequalities, or the US National Institute of Health-sponsored collaboration between the Icahn School of Medicine at Mount Sinai's and Tehran University to research patterns of cardiovascular disease—have been either "terminated or suspended" due to banks' refusals of assisting in transferring research or grant funding to Iran.[547] In 2016, researchers allocated 450 million rials to be used in 2019 for a project for human stem-cell therapies for spinal cord injuries. By the time 2019 came around, the budget had lost two-thirds of its value and the project was "almost a year behind schedule."[548]

The combination of secondary sanctions on banks and the drop in purchasing power of university budgets due to rial devaluation have eliminated Iranian academics' ability to pay for travel or equipment. One scientist said, "Being unable to do the simplest things, like ordering books online or paying registration fees for conferences, should speak volumes about the significance of being cut off from the international financial institutions." A human geneticist at Shiraz University seconded the sentiment: "The sanctions are affecting health, research and education, things that were not supposed to be their target. […] Planning a research study in any field of science seems to be almost impossible."[549]

Problems remain even when Iranian researchers are able to participate in exchange programs in the US. In 2019, Iranian researchers on exchange conducting stem-cell research in the US were arbitrarily arrested for "attempting to export chemicals [to Iran] … without obtaining permission from

547 Ibid.
548 Declan Butler, "How US sanctions are crippling science in Iran," *Nature*, 24 September, 2019.
549 Ibid.

the US Treasury Department." However, the growth factors that the researchers were carrying are used in medical research that, according to the defendants' lawyer, is not supposed to be subject to special authorization. These charges were eventually dropped by the US through a "prisoner swap" when Iran released an American academic it had imprisoned in retaliation.[550]

Not only are Iranian scientists being impacted by the sanctions, but US scientists are also being denied the ability to attend conferences in Iran—to the extent that American faculty have been blocked from traveling to Iran for research or scientific conferences.[551, 552] In 2017, a delegation of five US scientists planning to attend the 10th Annual Conference on Magnetic and Superconducting Materials in Tehran were "prohibited" by the United States' Office of Foreign Assets Control (OFAC) from traveling, with no explanation.[553] Pirouz Kavehpour, an Iranian American professor at UCLA, has similarly had to turn down several invitations to speak in Iran because he was simply "not allowed."[554]

Because of the "Brain Drain" and research limitations imposed by sanctions, many of Iran's top talents are leaving the country while those remaining are left with an academic system that needs development, updating, and funding.[555] Given this context, international collaborations would be

---

550 Michelle Catanzaro, "United States drop charges against two more scientists after Iran prisoner swap," *Nature*, 13 December 2019.

551 Levin, "Cut off from Family."

552 Butler, "How US sanctions."

553 Ibid.

554 Levin, "Cut off from Family."

555 Mohsen Tavakol, "Medical Education Under Economic Sanctions in Iran," *Academic Medicine* 84, no. 10 (October 2009): 1324.

instrumental in maintaining and improving the quality of Iran's education.[556]

Educational Programs and Opportunities

When sanctions were momentarily lifted, Iran "moved swiftly" to set up university collaborations with foreign institutions. Third-year Iranian undergraduates became eligible for Ph.D. programs in France, while French students were granted internship opportunities in Iran.[557] Slovakia established a partnership in science and technology with Iran. Iranian undergraduate students were given new study-abroad opportunities in Sweden and Cyprus, and exchange programs were also created for master's and doctoral programs.[558]

Nevertheless, American institutions remained risk-averse and restricted the kinds of subjects Iranian students were allowed to study—to the surprise of the US State Department. The University of Massachusetts (UMass) Amherst banned Iranians from studying "a range of engineering and natural science programs" for fear of using their skills to develop nuclear technology in Iran. However, many of the banned fields were unrelated to nuclear research, and 89 percent of Iranian students (many of whom are pursuing PhDs) hope to remain in the US after their degree. While UMass eventually

---

556 Hamid Mojtahedi, "Investing in Iran's Education Sector," Al Tamimi & Company, August 2016.

557 Chris Havergal, "Iran Sets up Europe HE Partnerships after Sanctions Lifted," Times Higher Education (THE), March 1, 2016.

558 Mojtahedi, "Investing in Iran's Education Sector."

removed the restriction, many other institutions have committed similar instances of "overcompliance."[559]

For instance, Kaplan "arbitrarily" banned Iranians from taking STEM courses because of sanctions, and students who had already taken the course were refused a completion certificate following the policy change.[560] Online education tools such as Coursera and edX have also barred Iranian students—the latter having to identify each individual Iranian resident on a platform of 17 million users and blocking their coursework based on IP address and profile information.[561, 562]

The cost of examination has also increased. "I wanted to pass the TOEFL or an IELTS," said Mori, who has considered immigrating to an English-speaking country. "I didn't do it last year and now I have to pay [at least three times] more. It's affecting everything, the sanctions."

US sanctions have not only negatively impacted Iran but have also "derailed scientific progress" by directly inhibiting collaborative opportunities between Iran and the rest of the world, and indirectly decreasing resource availability to Iranian researchers. Yet, the newest round of sanctions following withdrawal from the JCPOA has been particularly pernicious because the US government has "threatened criminal prosecution of US citizens, residents and scientists who collaborate with Iranian entities."[563] The "maximum pressure" crackdown on scientific research is not only detrimental to

559 Kaveh Madani and Khashayar Nikazmrad, "'Do-It-Yourself Sanctions Threaten Science Dialogue with Iran,'" *The Guardian*, February 23, 2015, sec. World news.

560 Dehghan, "Iranian Students Blocked."

561 Ibid.

562 "Sanctions Bar Educational Platform from Servicing Iranians," *National Iranian American Council (NIAC)* (blog), September 14, 2018.

563 Kokabisaghi et al., "Impact of United States Political Sanctions."

Iran and Iranian citizens, but also to the global community. Ali Gorji, an Iranian neuroscientist based in Germany, said, "The international scientific community needs to wake up to the problem and make more efforts to better support collaborative projects with their Iranian colleagues."[564]

***

Although this chapter is by no means extensive, it has hopefully shed light on some of the ways in which sanctions have impacted education. People in school and in research face political and economic barriers that prevent them from realizing their potential. Politicians and lawmakers should ensure that policies do not get in the way of human development and progress. People's right to education—as written in Article 26 of the Universal Declaration of Human Rights—should be supported and not made more difficult by international politics.

Regardless, there remains a lot that the international community may be able to do to support the Iranian people. Particularly as online-based resources become more available, there is an increasing number of ways institutions can support Iranian students and researchers who might not be able to travel for classes or conferences. Increased collaboration on non-sanctioned projects would give precedence to the peaceful exchange of information between countries as a means of strengthening Iran's relationships with the rest of the world. Although foreign institutions may be incentivized to be over-compliant, there is nevertheless a steep cost to exchanges forgone and meaningful partnerships abandoned.

---

564 Butler, "How US sanctions."

PART III

———

CHAPTER 9

ARTS

———

"Poetry occupies a particularly hallowed space in Iranian culture. Far from merely appreciating poetry as an art form, we Iranians—of all backgrounds and socio-economic classes—live and breathe it. A street sweeper will quote Khayyám on the transience of life, just as a taxi driver will recite the mystic verse of Rumi and a politician will invoke the patriotism of Ferdowsi. On the other hand, my great-uncle, just like Voltaire, loved the instructive Sa'di to the point that he chose our family name (Bekhrad, meaning 'wise') from a line in one of his poems."

—JOOBIN BEKHRAD[565]

Thus far, this book has examined situations where people's lives and living environment have been negatively impacted by economic sanctions. But it is important not to forget the

---

565 Joobin Bekhrad, "Iran's fascinating way to tell fortunes," BBC, 24 October 2018.

multidimensionality of the situation nor the agency of Iranian people. By briefly examining Iran's artistic heritage, this chapter will explore the existence of a culture of defiance and independent thinking that has empowered people to test the boundaries of what is permitted—whether that has been in the context of religion, state censorship, or sanctions.

Religion and State Censorship

The role of literature in Iranian culture cannot be overstated. At the tomb of Iran's most celebrated fourteenth-century poet, Hafez, one of the souvenirs that visitors may purchase is a two-book set: a book of the poet's writings and the Quran. Throughout the years, Hafez has become much more than a literary figure. Also known as the "Oracle of Shiraz," he is consulted by Iranians who seek answers to their life problems.[566] In a ritual known as *fal-e Hafez*, the answer-seeker asks their question silently, opens up the book of Hafez's writings to a random page, and the *ghazal* (love poem) on the page is supposed to provide Hafez's answers to the seeker's problems. On special occasions such as the Persian New Year, Hafez may also be consulted through this ritual, and the selected *ghazal* is read aloud to the entire gathering of friends and family.

Although religious restrictions may have had certain positive effects on creativity, there were also those who pushed against its strict demands. During his lifetime, Hafez was denounced by fundamentalist Muslims as a "hedonist who

---

566 Bekhrad, "Iran's fascinating way."

indulged in the pleasures of the earthly world."[567] Notwith-standing his eloquence and astute observations, part of his brilliance stems from his effortless transitions between "the serious and the scandalous," as well as the "exaltedly reli-gious and the sexily secular."[568] His poems sing "with para-mount passion of the ecstasy of love, the incomparable beauty of the beloved."[569] They celebrate wine and intoxication, and are critical of religious hypocrisy and false piety in a Muslim society. For instance, a line of one poem includes: "The sem-inary scholar was drunk yesterday and made a ruling/that wine is forbidden, but not so bad as [dipping into] the funds of religious endowments" (45.4; *faqih-e madrasa di mast bud o fatwā dād/ke mey ḥarām wali beh ze māl-e awqāf ast*)."[570] The admirable literary qualities of his writing are inextricable from his controversial subject matter.[571]

Even his pen-name, Hafez, is a play on words, meaning both a person who knows/recites the Quran by heart and a medieval musician (which is typically associated with riot-ous, religiously "immoral" behavior).[572] Hafez's work and his enduring popularity thereby reveal a delicate balance that challenges the religious tolerance of authority figures.

But poetry and literature are only samples of the art Iran has to offer; Iranians boast a cultural heritage of other arts and crafts, such as calligraphy, weaving, pottery, paint-ing, and metalwork. In spite of, or perhaps due to, certain

---

567 Hafez, Jahan Malek Khatun, and Obayd-e Zakani, *Faces of Love: Hafez and the Poets of Shiraz (Penguin Classics Deluxe Edition)* (Penguin, 2013).
568 Ibid.
569 Ehsan Yarshater, "HAFEZ i. AN OVERVIEW," *Encyclopaedia Iranica*, last updated March 1, 2012.
570 Ibid.
571 Ibid.
572 Ibid.

limitations, Persian art flourished. Because idolatry and the depiction of living beings are prohibited in Islamic art, Iranian artistic traditions after Islam centered around calligraphy, mathematics, and natural motifs.[573] For instance, intricate geometric patterns and tessellations emerged—including Penrose tiling, 500 years before it was named after the British mathematical physicist in the 1970s.[574]

***

While religious limitations persist in Iran's society today, many have become adept at navigating the push and pull of expression and restriction. As Jeremy Suyker writes in his article about Iran's underground art scene, "Iranian artists show formidable creativity and determination to cope with censorship. Tehran's art scene is growing fast, giving birth to new talent and producing inspiring works."[575] From fashion and music to film and literature, Iranian creatives have—whether intentionally or unintentionally—found ingenious ways of circumventing barriers and pushing for their voices to be heard.

In the capital, the fashion scene has been steadily growing. Whereas twenty years ago women were primarily seen wearing "dark colors and shapeless sacks," young women in Tehran today are not only wearing brighter colors, but their manner of dress has also changed. Instead of pants, leggings

573 Reza Sarhangi, "Persian Arts: A Brief Study," Visual Mathematics, accessed October 23, 2020.

574 Mehran Gharleghi, "How Iranian Architects Invented Ways to Stay Cool | British Council," British Council (blog), April 17, 2015.

575 Jeremy Suyker, "Iran's Underground Art Scene," Maptia, accessed October 23, 2020.

have become increasingly common, as well as "headscarves so minimal that they expose most of a woman's hair."[576] As of 2019, as many as five to ten fashion shows are being held per day in Tehran; local fashion labels are competing for greater shares of the Iranian market.[577]

When the police raided a fashion show in an affluent suburb of Tehran in 2019, it had been an intentional act by the event organizers. Models in the "big and flamboyant" fashion show were wearing wings and other accessories as part of a "fantasy-inspired" collection, which conservatives attacked as being un-Islamic, "resemb[ling] those of Satan worshippers."[578, 579] Because these clothes apparently "promot[ed] immorality," the Tehran police closed the site where the show was held, and the fashion label faced prosecution in court. Yet, the label had masterminded this publicity stunt: "They calculated that several days of store closure and millions of tomans[580] in fines were equivalent to the price of an ad campaign, but they never would have gotten the coverage without what happened," said one of the event organizers.[581] Using the repressive system to their advantage, the police raid had sparked coverage from both domestic and international media outlets.

Another example of creatives challenging Iranian authority is the underground rock band O-Hum. O-Hum performs

---

576 Barbara Slavin, "Iran Holds First Ever Fashion Week," Al-Monitor, March 27, 2015.

577 Ershad Alijani, "Iranian Label Accused of Organising 'un-Islamic' Fashion Show," The France 24 Observers, March 13, 2019.

578 Maryam Sinaiee, "Underground Designers Thriving In Iran's Fashion Market, Official Admits," Radio Farda, February 1, 2020.

579 Alijani, "Iranian Label Accused."

580 toman = 10 rial

581 Alijani, "Iranian Label Accused."

"Persian Rock": a combination of rock and traditional Iranian styles, using centuries-old poetry, primarily from Hafez, as lyrics. For Shahram Sharbaf, O-Hum's founder, Hafez's lyrics provide him a way of indirectly critiquing the current situation in Iran. "Names, times and countries change but some things never change. Especially in our country. I saw that he's saying exactly the same things I want to say, without me being in risk because I haven't written these [poems]," he said.[582] Lyrics in O-Hum songs include *"Vaezan ke in jelve dar mehrab o manbar mikonand, chon be khalvat miravand an kare digar mikonand"* ("On the pulpit, preachers, goodness display—Yet in private, they have a different way").[583] Although the band was initially rejected from obtaining a publication license by the Ministry of Culture and Islamic Guidance for its unconventional style, the band has since performed on many occasions both in Iran and internationally[584].

The celebrated filmmaker and recipient of the *Palme d'Or* at the Cannes Film Festival, Abbas Kiarostami, has also had several run-ins with the government regarding the publication of his work. *First Case, Second Case,* his documentary about a group of students getting in trouble at school, was awarded a prize at the Tehran Festival of Films for Children and Young Adults shortly before it was prohibited, presumably because many understood it to be a parable about the Shah's secret police. *Homework,* ostensibly about his sons' homework, was interpreted by some as a critique of Iran's education system. The movie was prohibited for three years before becoming available for adults. According to Ken Loach,

---

582 Farid Pazhoohi, "Interview with Shahram Sharbaf, Frontman of O-Hum: Part I," *Mideast Tunes* (blog), December 28, 2011.

583 Ibid.

584 Ibid.

a British director who had worked with Kiarostami, "It's the stories he has chosen that are the real political act." He continued, "those directors were choosing to make films about people who were not heroic but mundane, telling stories that were often comic. Like them, he is subtly subversive."[585]

Mahmoud Dowlatabadi, considered one of the most important writers in contemporary Iran, was arrested by the Shah's secret police in 1974. When he asked why he had been arrested, the police apparently acknowledged that he had not committed any offense, "but everyone we arrest seems to have copies of your novels, so that makes you provocative to revolutionaries."[586] Adept at depicting social and political upheaval, and drawing from his rural origins, Dowlatabadi's work "examine[s] the complexities and moral ambiguities of the experience of the poor and forgotten, mixing the brutality of that world with the lyricism of the Persian language."[587] Although many of his books have been published internationally and read in countries like the US, UK, and Germany, his works are still considered "subversive" in Iran. Among other notable works, Dowlatabadi wrote *The Colonel* in the 1980s about his interpretation of the revolution. When the Ministry of Culture and Islamic Guidance finally examined it to determine if it should be published in Iran, they found the narrative to be contrary to the regime's understanding of the revolution. "They didn't say yes, and they didn't say no. So, it's still stuck," said Dowlatabadi.[588]

---

585 Stuart Jeffries, "Landscapes of the Mind," *The Guardian*, April 16, 2005, sec. Film.
586 Larry Rohter, "An Iranian Storyteller's Personal Revolution," *The New York Times*, July 1, 2012, sec. Books.
587 Ibid.
588 Ibid.

Due to a variety of personal or political reasons, many Iranian artists no longer live in their home country. For instance, Marjane Satrapi, author of bestselling graphic novel *Persepolis* and co-director of the film with the same name, had moved from Tehran to Europe around the time of the revolution, where she now resides. Other artists have chosen to spend their entire lives in Iran. For the late Kiarostami, Iran was the setting for his best work. "When you take a tree that is rooted in the ground, and transfer it from one place to another, the tree will no longer bear fruit. And if it does, the fruit will not be as good as it was in its original place. If I had left my country, I would be the same as the tree," he explained.[589]

For the artists who remain in Iran, challenges to artistic expression are not limited to those imposed by the government. International sanctions and political tensions between Iran and other countries have also made it difficult for creatives to sustain their living.

Sanctions

"These sanctions have harmed art and culture more than the censorship inside the country," said the artist Tarlan Rafiee in disbelief.[590] She had needed twenty pieces of Fabriano Rosaspina, a special kind of paper used in printmaking, but because imported visual art equipment was in short supply in Iran, she was only able to purchase one piece from the art store in Tehran.

---

589 Jeffries, "Landscapes of the Mind."
590 Rebecca Anne Proctor, "For Years, Iran's Art Scene Has Been a Pioneer in the Mideast. Now US Sanctions Are Knocking Its Artists Back to the 18th Century," Artnet News, June 17, 2019.

Hormoz Hematian, the founder of the Tehran-based art gallery Dastan's Basement, shared the feeling that the sanctions were stifling creativity: "From the cost of materials and their availability to the increased living costs, it is not the best time for production."[591]

For those who have already sold artworks, international sanctions have made it extremely difficult for artists to receive the money: "Artists without international bank accounts must often pay additional fees to bring money in through so-called exchange companies. Artists with foreign bank accounts, meanwhile, struggle to cash checks abroad with Iranian passports. Sometimes, an artist will fly to collect the money from a gallery and bring it back to Iran physically."[592] One artist was apparently owed over $60,000 from having sold multiple artworks. Others, like Sahand Hesamiyan, were waiting for their art dealers to travel to Tehran to get paid.[593]

Art is supposedly classified as "informational material" and should be exempt from US sanctions. However, foreign firms and financial institutions remain risk-averse given the threat of secondary sanctions. According to the Swiss gallery, AB Fine Art AG, who had been late paying Iranian artists, "extreme regulations on the part of the banks in Switzerland" were the cause for delay.[594] Iranian collectors abroad have also faced problems sending money to the country. Fees going through exchange houses (that facilitate currency exchange) are so high that it was no longer deemed cost-effective for transactions under $20,000. "I cannot send money even from a UAE bank account abroad because I have an Iranian name,"

591 Ibid.
592 Ibid.
593 Ibid.
594 Ibid.

said an anonymous collector based in Dubai.[595] Instances of overcompliance were everywhere. A collector in Paris could not receive the artwork because the bank refused to pay the shipping company, after discovering the artist was Iranian: "their compliance team had Googled the artist and seen that he was originally from Iran."[596]

Galleries and art dealers abroad who chose to work with artists in Iran experienced stressful transaction situations. This kind of negative experience has deterred many from pursuing further collaboration. As the Swiss gallery's co-founder Franz Leupi stated, "In the future, we will no longer work with artists from Iran." Shirin Partovi, founder and director of the Shirin Art Gallery in Tehran similarly described Iran's isolation: "We have no clients abroad due to the sanctions. We have local clients only."[597] Real and perceived barriers therefore make it especially difficult for Iranian artists to engage with the international market. As the Geneva-based art consultant, Dina Nasser-Khadivi says, Iranian people have to "work ten times harder to find legal loopholes in order to get things done," if the opportunity is available.[598]

Exhibiting artwork in art fairs has also become a major challenge. To prepare for Iran's pavilion at the Venice Biennale, the Tehran-based Curator Ali Bakhtiari had to pay his staff, for his hotel room, and all other expenses during his trip in cash because Iranian bank accounts cannot be used abroad. It took him a month to find an insurance company willing to work with him. For other artists and art dealers, the devalued rial means that accommodation, food, and

---

595 Ibid.
596 Ibid.
597 Ibid.
598 Ibid.

other items abroad become more expensive. Moreover, security checks for Iranian shipments may cause delays in receiving the works. Staff and artists are also often denied visas.[599]

At the height of Iranian theater productions, there were as many as 148 performances daily. Privately-run theaters had been popping up in the country's capital, accounting for almost two-thirds of Tehran's theaters. But because basic goods have become much more expensive for ordinary people, there has been a significant decline in people attending theater performances. Whereas in 2016, performances would be sold out and people were willing to pay to sit on the floor, by 2019, sanctions and increased government crackdown forced many theaters to the brink of closure. "Theatre in general is going down both in quality and quantity," said Mostafa Kooshki, director of the Mostaghel theater. "The economic hardships do not let artists share thoughts like [they did] two years ago and be creative."[600] According to a professor of cinema at a university in Tehran, the worsening condition for theater is due to both materialistic and psychological effects of sanctions: "The decline in the number of theatre and cinema goers is both related to economic pressure as well as a sense of despair in society. Even cinema students do not seriously follow or take part in events on art movies and documentaries."[601]

Economic sanctions have also negatively impacted the film industry. Because secondary sanctions have hindered money transfer to and from Iranian banks, they have deterred firms in other countries from collaborating with

---

599 Ibid.

600 Monavar Khalaj, "Curtain Comes down on Iran's Theatre Boom," *Financial Times*, January 11, 2019.

601 Ibid.

the Iranian film industry. Iranian producers have also been less interested in investing in productions with foreign countries.[602] Not only that, but domestic film production has also sharply declined. According to Mohammad Attebai, a film distributor and cinema consultant, the "first clear impact of the sanctions that we can see" is the 31 percent drop in film production since the reimposition of US sanctions.[603]

The decrease in production may be partially attributed to the ballooning film budgets as a consequence of rapid inflation. For Behnam Behzadi, whose film *Inversion* had been screened at the 2016 Cannes Film Festival, the budget of his film *I'm Scared* increased from $550,000 to $780,000 in 2019. "If he had started production now, he would not have been able to complete it," said the sales agent and producer, Katayoon Shahabi.[604]

She continued, "The economic situation is a disaster for independent cinema." Not only has funding become harder, but selling Iranian films to other countries has also become more difficult. "It's basically impossible to sell to any country, not just to the US," she said, citing money transfer as a particular obstacle, "Companies that work with Iranians are penalized, so they don't want to take any risks." Echoing the sentiments of art dealers, Iranians working in the film industry also complain of not being able to attend foreign film festivals, award ceremonies, or promotional events: "Anybody in this business has to have a bank account or a company

---

602 "Shahram Mokri: Iran Sanctions Big Obstacle to Joint Film Projects," Tehran Times, September 8, 2020.

603 Nick Vivarelli, "U.S. Pressure, Sanctions on Iran Take Toll on Its Film Industry," Variety, May 19, 2019.

604 Ibid.

outside Iran. Otherwise, simply, you can't sell movies, or even pay for your expenses while attending markets."[605]

Despite, or perhaps motivated by, isolation from the international community, Iranian artists are determined to contribute to arts and culture both domestically and globally. As articulated by Ali Bakhtiari, curator for the Venice Biennale, every presentation of Iran to the world is consequential: "We have been labeled as terrorists by the US government and it was very important to exhibit in Venice with a message of peace and a belief in a better future."[606] Art Consultant Dina Nasser-Khadivi shared this sentiment, "The really sad thing for me is to witness how the word 'Iran' has often become a synonym for paranoia."[607] Yet, the desire to be appreciated remains, and signs of persistence are everywhere. "We want the international art community to understand that we are all working so hard. [...] To say the Iran game is over is not going to happen. We are going to keep going," said Hormoz Hematian.[608] Actor Babak Karimi echoed this sentiment: "We are so used to living in instability and uncertainty," he said, but "filmmakers continue to work as they always did."[609]

When the JCPOA was first announced, there had been a wave of optimism that spread across Iran. In an interview with France 24 in 2016, the rock musician King Raam exuded optimism. "The environment has become a lot more relaxed; I find. Despite the limitations that exist, to me Tehran is this sort of new New York," he said. "It has this really intense creative buzz about it, and I think we're at this tipping point

---

605 Ibid.
606 Proctor, "Iran's Art Scene."
607 Ibid.
608 Ibid.
609 Vivarelli, "U.S. Pressure."

between now and the next few years and opening up the doors with the West, you know, sure enough, the next several years we're going to close this gap and become even more globalized."[610]

***

Arguably, artists interact with and test the boundaries of domestic and international regulatory constraints more often than most ordinary citizens. Their actions may more clearly reveal Iranian people's ability to tolerate complexity and adapt to difficult situations. Whether it is freedom of expression or economic sanctions, they are not deterred by these seemingly overwhelming obstacles. On certain occasions—such as in the case of the fashion shows—they have even used these barriers to their advantage.

But make no mistake: this resilience, creativity, and tenacity exemplified by Iranian creatives when confronting challenges are present throughout Iranian society, as evidenced by the previous chapters. Although the art scene makes up a small fraction of overall Iranian society, the abundance of talent provides a glimpse of what the international community may be forgoing by limiting opportunities to Iranian people as a whole.

More specifically, reincorporating Iran with the international community would provide unprecedented opportunities for informational exchange. Iranian arts and culture would finally be appreciated in a way that they deserve, and foreign companies would find a new and foreign market that

---

610 *France 24 English*, "Iran: Lifting the veil on Tehran's cultural life", January 12, 2016, video, 11:25.

would provide unique opportunities. When designer Sharif Razavi was asked in 2015 whether he thought Americans would buy Iranian clothing if they were granted the opportunity to do so, he replied "100 percent."[611]

For those working under existing conditions, they have no choice but to navigate the added obstacles imposed by sanctions. The talent and determination that Iranian people possess could be used in much more productive ways— instead of spending a month looking for an insurance company to cover the shipment of artworks for the Venice Biennale as Ali Bakhtiari did, for instance. While the United States ostensibly values freedom of speech and expression, their sanctions impede Iranians from doing so by limiting the supply of materials and equipment, restricting funding, and hindering cross-country collaboration. The opportunity costs of comprehensive sanctions to the international community should not be overlooked.

---

611 Slavin, "Iran Holds First Ever Fashion Week."

CONCLUSION

———

*"I don't think Americans know very much about our country.
All this talk about regional power and nuclear arms—that's
politicians talking. No one listens to them. We're really a very
simple people—like Americans."*

—MEHRAD, AN IRANIAN TOUR GUIDE[612]

When I traveled to Iran with my two friends, none of us could
have known what it was actually like. Elements of Western
influence were everywhere—as evidenced by Iranians saying
"merci" and using other French words in everyday conversation. Even though Islam had been introduced to the Per-
sians 1,500 years ago, Iranian people still see their identity
as "nothing like the Arab world": they are ethnically distinct,
speak Farsi instead of Arabic, practice a branch of Islam
different than that of most Arab countries, and live within

---

612 Christopher Thornton, "The Iran We Don't See: A Tour of the Country
Where People Love Americans," *The Atlantic*, June 6, 2012.

a different culture.[613] Having once been one of the greatest civilizations in the world, Iranian people are understandably proud of their heritage, and many traditions continue to be practiced today. At the same time, many people embrace the new and are up to date with the latest global developments, often getting their information from social media (as of 2018, Instagram and WhatsApp were not banned). It was not at all the dangerous country that we had expected it to be, based on the "do not travel" warnings placed by many foreign countries—not just the US.

But, more than anything we observed about this complicated country, we experienced immense kindness and generosity from the locals who went out of their way to make sure that we were welcome in their country. From our interactions and conversations, it became clear that these people's hopes and dreams were not much different from my own. In the words of my friend Koohyar, "Iran is the same as other countries. People basically like the same things: to be happy, to have fun, to do interesting things, have a good life… It would be nice if people think more positively about Iran."

Unfortunately, decades of sanctions have made life in Iran more difficult and unpredictable. For more vulnerable sections of the population, sanctions have prevented people from obtaining lifesaving medicine, or made it too expensive to afford food. People are driven into selling their homes or raising children in neighborhoods ridden with social problems. Education becomes a luxury when kids have to contribute to the family income and school supplies are unaffordable. As Sussan Tahmasebi, the director of FEMENA, which supports women human rights defenders, articulated:

---

613 Ibid.

"While the [US] administration claims that sanctions are targeting those in power, the sanctions really impact the ordinary people, especially women, children, minorities, refugees, the disabled, and the sick. Sanctions have become a method of warfare, denying life-saving medicines to sick people, destroying livelihoods and plunging millions into poverty. [...] Most of those who have lost employment or who have suffered economically were already working in the economic margins. They were employed as day laborers or street peddlers, or providers of services. They were women-headed households, who despite low wages are responsible for entire families."[614]

The US—which prides itself on the protection of civil liberties by condemning human rights abuses around the world—is itself a perpetrator of human rights violations in Iran.

Though some people may have been hit particularly hard by the economic sanctions, to varying degrees, ordinary Iranian citizens have all been negatively impacted. At a minimum, the sudden and drastic changes to the economy from political decisions have damaged people's ability to plan for the long-term—whether that's for starting a business or purchasing a home. Scientists, artists, students, and others have likewise felt the negative impact of sanctions on their lives. Career and educational advancement opportunities become limited because people cannot study abroad, pay for research equipment, or attend international exhibitions.

---

614 Madea Benjamin and Sussan Tahmasebi, "Iranian Women Squeezed by US Sanctions, COVID-19 and their Government," Common Dreams, published on May 14, 2020.

When we spoke, Mori told me, "In the past seven or eight years, it [has been a] struggle to figure out what's going on in Iran. It's affecting my life, and I'm really tired. I want to go somewhere and live and not have to think about what the government is doing... I'm just tired, my mind is tired." The weariness was clear in his voice. "I made perfect plans for my business and I was doing perfectly, and I was successful... I don't complain, but if we had a better relationship with the rest of the world, it would be much easier. They cut off our connection with the rest of the world and it's not our choice."

To think that the damage is confined within the borders of Iran is also false. Iran's environmental degradation and air pollution affect the global ecosystem and directly contribute to climate change. Critically endangered species only found in Iran cannot be properly protected. Moreover, restricting exchange between Iran and the international community is costly. Not only are people missing out on the intangible benefits such as understanding a different culture or peoples, but sanctions also cost foreign companies hundreds of billions of dollars in exports foregone or joint projects abandoned.

This book does not go into detail about the effectiveness of sanctions on Iran, nor does it discuss in length how poor government policies have contributed to sanctions' unequal impacts on ordinary citizens. Nevertheless, it has hopefully demonstrated that sanctions are inherently problematic and infringe on the human rights of Iranian people. By doing so, the book has aimed to raise questions about whether sanctions are the appropriate policy tool in this context. Is it really impossible to prevent Iran from acquiring a nuclear weapon, to deter its support for terrorist groups, or to condemn its human rights violations, without first harming the Iranian people?

"In this game it's only Iranian people who lose; who live under pressure," said K, who lives in Tehran. "The instability last year, it was very crazy—it's like you cannot plan your life, you cannot know what to do with your life because everything is changing, businesses are changing... Any plan you make can be affected. This is not healthy you know; they're destroying the nation! It's selfish from both governments, and between them, nobody cares about Iranian people."

What You Can Do to Help

For politicians

Currently, human rights concerns do not seem to be sufficiently incorporated into the policymaking process. Despite claims that humanitarian aid is exempt from sanctions, this book has hopefully shown that this does not seem to be the case in practice, and Iranian people's human rights are not properly respected. Establishing a norm that places greater emphasis on adopting non-invasive strategies, such as using diplomacy or other negotiation tactics, and avoiding using sanctions as a means of political signaling (to a domestic audience, for instance) would reduce the possibility of inflicting further unintended harm.

Rather than using threats and coercion when dealing with Iran, recognizing and addressing the regime's perception of external threats as well as its core domestic issues could encourage a foundation of trust between negotiating parties. This is essential for restarting negotiations, especially because the US had reneged on its previous Iran strategy by exiting the JCPOA. By demanding the removal of sanctions, Iran desires—or at the very least, accepts—that sanctions relief would entail reintegration with the international community. Fostering this kind of trade and exchange could increase the country's incentives to cooperate with its trading partners. Strengthening Iran's trade dependence is important for the West, not only because it helps tie Iranian interests to those of liberal societies, but also because it opens up the range of policy tools that can be used in the future, if necessary.

The United States, as an advocate for democracy and human rights, has a responsibility to act consistently and diplomatically with other countries. Re-evaluating decades-old foreign policy positions and attempting to shift away from them may be difficult in practice, but doing so would command respect from the international community.

For the General Public

Based on the US political system, public perception and government policy are mutually reinforcing—government officials design policy platforms based on the opinions of its voter base, and the people often form judgments about foreign policy based on the rhetoric of their policymakers. The American public therefore has an important voice that has the potential to influence policy decisions. By understanding that Iran is more complex than merely being "the enemy" and urging policymakers to pay greater attention to humanitarian consequences, people have the ability to shift America's policy focus from an antagonistic perspective that presumes Iran's irrationality to one that addresses the regime's core strategic interests. Generating negative public attention on hostile US policy strategies, such as comprehensive sanctions, may hopefully compel policymakers to consider other tools that inflict less collateral damage.

Beyond influencing policy, there are also smaller ways to humanize the Iranian people. Learning about the country beyond the images of the regime typically depicted in Western media, supporting Iranian artists and creatives, and thinking critically about policy externalities are all possible ways to foster a nuanced understanding of Iran. For those looking for further resources, organizations such as the Human Rights Watch, or the Center for Human Rights in Iran, have written extensively about human rights related issues in Iran, including sanctions. Think-tanks like the Atlantic Council or Council on Foreign Relations bring more policy-oriented perspectives to the sanctions issue. Other special-interest publications such as *Artnet* or *Science Magazine* have also included articles about sanctions' effects on art and science, respectively. Radio Farda, BBC Persian, and other international news agencies such as *The Guardian*, and *Reuters* provide wide coverage of Iran while remaining independent from government influences. Those who would like to actively contribute could raise awareness or support the work of nonprofits such as the Center for Human Rights in Iran, Amnesty International, or other focus-specific organizations such as FEMENA, which aims to support women human rights defenders in the Middle East and North African regions, or the Norwegian Refugee Council (NRC), which provides basic humanitarian services to displaced Afghans in Iran and supports their Iranian host communities.[615, 616]

---

615 "FEMENA Home Page," FEMENA, accessed October 23, 2020, https://femena.net/.
616 "NRC in Iran," Norwegian Refugee Council, accessed October 22, 2020.

When we spoke, A had this to say: "Most Europeans and Americans think Iranians are terrorists, but it's not true. If they want to learn about Iran and about Persia, they can read history, they can come to Iran, and watch some documentaries to know us better. Because as you know, most Iranians are really welcoming, they love having guests. They are peaceful, they are warm. But you don't hear these things on the news. If people could come here and see from near how we are doing, then maybe it would be the best way."

As evidenced by the dramatic changes of approval ratings for Iran and the US towards each other in the past decades, public perception is malleable. Maybe shifting domestic perspectives and demands can spark renewed, constructive dialogue between America and Iran.

ACKNOWLEDGEMENTS

I'd like to acknowledge those who have supported me with through this crazy, intense process:

Candy Chan, Nicolas Le Toux, my travel buddies Nicolas Wong and Alfred Helskog, Developmental Editor Cassandra Caswell, Marketing Editor Chelsea Friday, Adrienne Zhang, Rachelle Hung, Marieta Rojas, Justin Leung, Pranav Nanga, Anna Bakwin, Rachel Hu, Henry Fung, Nicholas Foo, Martin Shi, Sarah Ding, Teddy Knox and Ada Fan for supporting the earlier versions of this idea, and Professor Marvin Zonis for answering all my email questions.

I'd also like to gratefully acknowledge those who have shaped my Iranian experience:

Koohyar, Mori, and the anonymous Iranian friends who helped answer all my questions and showed me their beautiful country, the friends I made in the hostels, and the French lady who yelled at Nicolas and Alfred.

Lastly, I'd like to acknowledge a few sources of inspiration:

Michael Axworthy, Samantha Power, and Ali Vaez

APPENDIX

Introduction

Amnesty International. "Saudi Arabia 2019." Accessed October 21, 2020. https://www.amnesty.org/en/countries/middle-east-and-north-africa/saudi-arabia/report-saudi-arabia/.

Associated Press. "Iran 'launches military satellite into orbit' amid tension with US." *The Telegraph*, April 22, 2020. https://www.telegraph.co.uk/news/2020/04/22/iran-launches-military-satellite-orbit-amid-tensions-us/.

Axworthy, Michael. *Revolutionary Iran: A History of the Islamic Republic*. Oxford University Press, 2013.

CNN Money. "The world's priciest foods." CNN. Last updated July 23, 2008. https://money.cnn.com/galleries/2008/fsb/0807/gallery.most_expensive_foods.fsb/4.html.

Digital image, Imgflip, accessed October 22, 2020. https://imgflip.com/i/347we7.

Digital image, Reddit, accessed October 22, 2020. https://preview.redd.it/hkcv3w583tt21.png?width=454&format=png&auto=webp&s=9d6e7b592d9ba43e4bce9a83ce-50d7385ad51ff9.

Freedom House. "Saudi Arabia." Accessed October 21, 2020. https://freedomhouse.org/country/saudi-arabia/freedom-world/2020.

"Iran, Islamic Republic Of: Country-Specific: Arrivals of Non-Resident Visitors at National Borders, by Nationality 2014-2018 (07.2019)." *UNWTO World Tourism Organization*, October 16, 2019. https://doi.org/10.5555/unwtotfb0364012120142018201907.

Rasmussen Reports. "Voters See Economic Sanctions As An Effective Response," July 26, 2017. https://www.rasmussenreports.com/public_content/politics/general_politics/july_2017/voters_see_economic_sanctions_as_an_effective_response.

Reiss, Megan. "Americans Support Sanctions … Most of the Time." Lawfare, January 22, 2018. https://www.lawfareblog.com/americans-support-sanctions-most-time-0.

"Trump Button," Digital image, Imgflip, accessed October 22, 2020. https://imgflip.com/i/2lubky.

Trump, Donald (@realDonaldTrump). Twitter. November 2, 2018. 11:01 a.m. Accessed October 22, 2020. https://twitter.com/realDonaldTrump/status/1058388700617498625/photo/1.

United Nations. "Universal Declaration of Human Rights," October 6, 2015. https://www.un.org/en/universal-declaration-human-rights/.

Chapter 1: How we got here and preconceptions

Arablouei, Ramtin, and Rund Abdelfatah. "Four Days In August." July 11, 2019. *Throughline*. Podcast, 38:00. Accessed October 23, 2020. https://www.npr.org/2019/07/10/740510559/four-days-in-august.

Arsalai, Mohammed Harun, and Wil Patrick. "Iran's Shifting Afghan Alliances Don't Fit Easy Narratives," February 18, 2020.

https://foreignpolicy.com/2020/02/18/suleimani-war-quds-iran-shifting-afghan-alliances-dont-fit-easy-narratives/.

Axworthy, Michael. *Revolutionary Iran: A History of the Islamic Republic*. Oxford University Press, 2013.

Cameron, Adam. "The Artful Dodger: Iranian Tarof and Nuclear Negotiations." *The Guardian*, November 20, 2014, sec. World news. https://www.theguardian.com/world/iran-blog/2014/nov/20/-sp-iran-nuclear-negotiations-tarof.

Central Intelligence Agency. "The World Factbook—Middle East: Iran." Accessed October 21, 2020. https://www.cia.gov/library/publications/the-world-factbook/geos/ir.html.

Chris Matthews: Iran Will Remember What the United States Did. MSNBC, January 10, 2020. https://www.msnbc.com/hardball/watch/chris-matthews-iran-will-remember-what-the-united-states-did-76462661636.

Christopher de Bellaigue. "Talk Like an Iranian." The Atlantic, August 22, 2012. https://www.theatlantic.com/magazine/archive/2012/09/talk-like-an-iranian/309056/.

Cohen, Ryan. "Rhinoplasty and the Roosari from Ancient Persia to Modern Day Iran." Hektoen International: A Journal of Medical Humanities, Summer 2015. https://hekint.org/2017/01/22/rhinoplasty-and-the-roosari-from-ancient-persia-to-modern-day-iran/.

Cordesman, Anthony H. "The Crisis in Iran: What Now?" Center For Strategic & International Studies (CSIS), January 11, 2018. https://www.csis.org/analysis/crisis-iran-what-now.

Davis, Rowenna. "Nose No Problem." New Statesman, March 6, 2008. https://www.newstatesman.com/society/2008/03/nose-iran-religious-lenehan.

Eid, Mahmoud. "Perceptions about Muslims in Western Societies." In *Re-Imagining the Other*, edited by Mahmoud Eid and Karim H. Karim, 99-119. New York: Palgrave Macmillan, 2014.

Encyclopedia Britannica. "Mohammad Mosaddegh." Accessed October 21, 2020. https://www.britannica.com/biography/ Mohammad-Mosaddegh.

Encyclopaedia Iranica. "Persepolis," August 15, 2009. https://iranicaonline.org/articles/persepolis.

Gallagher, Nancy, Ebrahim Mohseni, and Clay Ramsay. "Iranian Public Opinion under 'Maximum Pressure.'" The Center for International and Security Studies at Maryland (CISSM), October 2019. https://worldpublicopinion.net/ wp-content/uploads/2019/12/Iranian_PO_under_Maximum_ Pressure_101819.pdf.

Harney, John. "How Do Sunni and Shia Islam Differ? (Published 2016)." The New York Times, January 3, 2016, sec. World. https://www.nytimes.com/2016/01/04/world/middleeast/q- and-a-how-do-sunni-and-shia-islam-differ.html.

Hart, Jo-Anne. "Perceptions and Courses of Actions toward Iran." Military Review 85, no. 14 (October 2005): 13.

History.com Editors. "Persian Empire." HISTORY, September 30, 2019. https://www.history.com/topics/ancient-middle-east/ persian-empire.

"Iran Oil: New Field with 53bn Barrels Found—Rouhani." BBC News, November 10, 2019, sec. Middle East. https://www.bbc.com/news/world-middle-east-50365235.

Jaafari, Shirin. "The Persian Art of Declining What You Really Want and Offering What You'll Never Give Could Play a Role in US-Iran Nuclear Talks." The World from PRX, November 5, 2014. https://www.pri.org/stories/2014-11-05/persian-art-declining- what-you-really-want-and-offering-what-youll-never-give.

Jones, Seth G. "Iran's Protests and the Threat to Domestic Stability." Center For Strategic & International Studies (CSIS), November 8, 2019. https://www.csis.org/analysis/irans-protests-and- threat-domestic-stability.

———. "War by Proxy: Iran's Growing Footprint in the Middle East." Center For Strategic & International Studies (CSIS), March 11, 2019. https://www.csis.org/war-by-proxy.

Lipka, Michael. "Muslims and Islam: Key Findings in the U.S. and around the World." *Pew Research Center* (blog), August 9, 2017. https://www.pewresearch.org/fact-tank/2017/08/09/muslims-and-islam-key-findings-in-the-u-s-and-around-the-world/.

Makovsky, Michael, and Jonathan Ruhe. "The Right Strategy for Iran Isn't Regime Change. It's Regime Collapse." The Washington Post, January 8, 2020. https://www.washingtonpost.com/opinions/2020/01/08/right-strategy-iran-isnt-regime-change-its-regime-collapse/.

Maleki, Abbas, and John Tirman, eds. *U.S.-Iran Misperceptions: A Dialogue*. 1st ed. Bloomsbury, 2014.

Maloney, Suzanne, and Keian Razipour. "The Iranian Revolution—A Timeline of Events." Brookings, January 24, 2019. https://www.brookings.edu/blog/order-from-chaos/2019/01/24/the-iranian-revolution-a-timeline-of-events/.

Moore, James. "The Sunni and Shia Schism: Religion, Islamic Politics, and Why Americans Need to Know the Differences." *The Social Studies* 106, no. 5 (September 3, 2015): 226-35. https://doi.org/10.1080/00377996.2015.1059794.

Niknam, Azadeh. "The Islamization of Law in Iran: A Time of Disenchantment." Middle East Research and Information Project (MERIP), Fall 1999. https://merip.org/1999/09/the-islamization-of-law-in-iran/.

Nima, Adena. "Iranian Students in 10 Universities Protest Regime's Nov Crackdown." Iran News Wire, December 7, 2019. https://irannewswire.org/iranian-students-in-10-universities-protest-regimes-nov-crackdown/.

Olson, Tyler. "Pompeo Accuses Iran of Echoing 'Hitler's Call for Genocide' over 'Final Solution' Rhetoric." Fox News, May 22,

2020. https://www.foxnews.com/politics/pompeo-accuses-iran-of-echoing-hilters-call-for-genocide-over-final-solution-rhetoric.

Oriental Institute at The University of Chicago. "Persepolis and Ancient Iran: The Apadana." Accessed October 21, 2020. https://oi.uchicago.edu/collections/photographic-archives/persepolis/apadana.

Patrikarakos, David. "Analysis: Iran's Younger Generation Positioned To Restore Political Roar." RadioFreeEurope Radio-Liberty (RFE/RL), May 18, 2017. https://www.rferl.org/a/iran-youth-positioned-to-restore-political-roar/28495856.html.

Pew Research Center: Global Attitudes & Trends. "Global Views of Iran Overwhelmingly Negative," June 11, 2013. https://www.pewresearch.org/global/2013/06/11/global-views-of-iran-overwhelmingly-negative/.

Radio Farda. "Iran Poll Shows Only 15 Percent In Tehran Satisfied With Government," December 22, 2019. https://en.radiofarda.com/a/iran-poll-shows-only-15-percent-in-tehran-satisfied-with-government/30338976.html.

Shahghasemi, Ehsan, D. Ray Heisey, and Goudarz Mirani. "How Do Iranians and U.S. Citizens Perceive Each Other: A Systematic Review." *Journal of Intercultural Communication*, no. 27 (November 2011). https://www.immi.se/intercultural/nr27/shahghasemi.htm.

Shahi, Afshin, and Ehsan Abdoh-Tabrizi. "Iran's 2019-2020 Demonstrations: The Changing Dynamics of Political Protests in Iran." *Asian Affairs* 51, no. 1 (January 2, 2020): 1-41. https://doi.org/10.1080/03068374.2020.1712889.

Shahidsaless, Shahir. "For Iran, Retaliation Is More than a Matter of Saving Face." Middle East Eye, January 8, 2020. http://www.middleeasteye.net/opinion/how-will-iran-retaliate-against-us-soleimanis-assassination.

———. "Why Europe Is Turning against US Policy on Syria and
Iran." Middle East Eye, November 6, 2018.
https://www.middleeasteye.net/opinion/why-europe-turning-
against-us-policy-syria-and-iran.

Stone, Richard. "New Tensions Dim Hopes for Salvaging Iran
Nuclear Deal." Science, June 17, 2020.
https://www.sciencemag.org/news/2020/06/new-tensions-dim-
hopes-salvaging-iran-nuclear-deal.

The National. "Iran Leaps into World's Top 10 Countries Performing Plastic Surgery," January 4, 2016.
https://www.thenationalnews.com/arts-culture/iran-leaps-
into-world-s-top-10-countries-performing-plastic-surgery-
1.174897.

Thornton, Christopher. "The Iran We Don't See: A Tour of the Country Where People Love Americans." The Atlantic, June 6, 2012.
https://www.theatlantic.com/international/archive/2012/06/
the-iran-we-dont-see-a-tour-of-the-country-where-people-
love-americans/258166/.

United States Institue of Peace: The Iran Primer. "Fact Sheet: Protests in Iran (1979-2019)," January 21, 2020.
https://iranprimer.usip.org/blog/2019/dec/05/fact-sheet-
protests-iran-1999-2019-0.

Valle, Julihana. "The Persian Art of Etiquette." BBC Travel, November 14, 2016. https://www.bbc.com/travel/story/20161104-the-
persian-art-of-etiquette.

Wagner, Meg, Ivana Kottasová, Mike Hayes, Veronia Rocha, and
Fernando Alfonso III. "Iran Attacks Bases Housing US Troops."
CNN, January 9, 2020. https://www.cnn.com/middleeast/live-
news/us-iran-news-01-08-2020/index.html.

World Bank. "Islamic Republic of Iran." Accessed October 21, 2020.
https://www.worldbank.org/en/country/iran.

Wynarczyk, Natasha. "These Persian Girls Are Inciting a National Debate Around Nose Jobs." Vice, December 14, 2015. https://www.vice.com/en/article/785y3x/persian-women-against-the-nose-job.

Chapter 2: What are sanctions?

Amnesty International. "Iran 2019." Accessed October 21, 2020. https://www.amnesty.org/en/countries/middle-east-and-north-africa/iran/report-iran/.

Braverman, Burt, and Dsu-Wei Yuen. "EU Companies Face Tough Choice: Violate U.S. Secondary Sanctions on Iran or Amended EU Blocking Regulations." *Lexology.* Accessed October 21, 2020. https://www.lexology.com/library/detail.aspx?g=fd-c7f000-feec-4e71-99ce-efbdc17efe15.

Bob Menendez for Senate. "Menendez, Kirk Amendment for Stronger Sanctions Against Iran Passes Unanimously in the Senate," December 1, 2011. https://www.menendez.senate.gov/newsroom/press/menendez-kirk-amendment-for-stronger-sanctions-against-iran-passes-unanimously-in-the-senate.

Center for Economic and Social Rights (CESR). "What Are Economic, Social and Cultural Rights?," December 3, 2008. https://www.cesr.org/what-are-economic-social-and-cultural-rights.

Davenport, Kelsey. "Implementation of the Joint Plan of Action At A Glance." Arms Control Association (ACA), August 2017. https://www.armscontrol.org/Implementation-of-the-Joint-Plan-of-Action-At-A-Glance.

———. "UN Security Council Resolutions on Iran." Arms Control Association, August 2017. https://www.armscontrol.org/factsheets/Security-Council-Resolutions-on-Iran.

Economist, The. "America Must Use Sanctions Cautiously," May 17, 2018. https://www.economist.com/leaders/2018/05/17/america-must-use-sanctions-cautiously.

Encyclopedia Britannica. "Mohammad Reza Shah Pahlavi." Accessed October 21, 2020. https://www.britannica.com/biography/Mohammad-Reza-Shah-Pahlavi#ref343725.

Encyclopedia Britannica. "Ruhollah Khomeini." Accessed October 21, 2020. https://www.britannica.com/biography/Ruhollah-Khomeini.

Escribà-Folch, Abel, and Joseph Wright. "Dealing with Tyranny: International Sanctions and the Survival of Authoritarian Rulers." *International Studies Quarterly* 54, no. 2 (2010): 335-59.

Forrer, John. "Economic Sanctions: Sharpening a Vital Foreign Policy Tool." *Atlantic Council,* June 2017. https://www.atlanticcouncil.org/wp-content/uploads/2017/06/Economic_Sanctions_web_0614.pdf.

Gilsinan, Kathy. "A Boom Time for U.S. Sanctions." *The Atlantic,* May 3, 2019. https://www.theatlantic.com/politics/archive/2019/05/why-united-states-uses-sanctions-so-much/588625/.

Global Policy Forum. "Criticism of the Sanctions." Accessed November 9, 2020. https://www.globalpolicy.org/security-council/index-of-countries-on-the-security-council-agenda/sanctions/case-study-sanctions-against-iraq/42021.html.

Gupta, A. K. "Iraq: 'Smart Sanctions' Still Kill." *Global Policy Forum,* July 2002. https://www.globalpolicy.org/component/content/article/170/42205.html.

Gözler Çamur, Elif. "Civil and Political Rights vs. Social and Economic Rights: A Brief Overview." *Journal of Bitlis Eren University Institute of Social Sciences* 6, no. 1 (2017): 205-14.

Haass, Richard N. "Economic Sanctions: Too Much of a Bad Thing." Brookings (blog), June 1, 1998. https://www.brookings.edu/research/economic-sanctions-too-much-of-a-bad-thing/.

Hakimian, Hassan. How Sanctions Affect Iran's Economy. Interview by Toni Johnson, May 22, 2012. https://www.cfr.org/interview/how-sanctions-affect-irans-economy.

———. "Seven Key Misconceptions about Economic Sanctions." World Economic Forum, May 9, 2019. https://www.weforum.org/agenda/2019/05/seven-fallacies-of-economic-sanctions/.

How Saddam Happened (2002). https://fas.org/irp/congress/2002_cr/s092002.html.

Hufbauer, Gary Clyde. Sanctions on Iran: Why They Worked and Why a "Snapback" May Not Work. Interview by Steve Weisman, March 2, 2016. https://www.piie.com/experts/peterson-perspectives/sanctions-iran-why-they-worked-and-why-snapback-may-not-work.

Katzman, Kenneth. "Iran Sanctions." *Congressional Research Service*, July 23, 2020. https://fas.org/sgp/crs/mideast/RS20871.pdf.

Landler, Mark. "Trump Abandons Iran Nuclear Deal He Long Scorned (Published 2018)." *The New York Times*, May 8, 2018, sec. World. https://www.nytimes.com/2018/05/08/world/middleeast/trump-iran-nuclear-deal.html.

Lindsay, James M. "Trade Sanctions as Policy Instruments: A Re-Examination." *International Studies Quarterly* 30, no. 2 (June 1, 1986): 153-73. https://doi.org/10.2307/2600674.

Lynch, Colum. "Despite U.S. Sanctions, Iran Expands Its Nuclear Stockpile." *Foreign Policy*, May 8, 2020. https://foreignpolicy.com/2020/05/08/iran-advances-nuclear-program-withdrawal-jcpoa/.

Manson, Katrina. "What the US Withdrawal from the Iran Nuclear Deal Means." *The Financial Times*, May 9, 2018. https://www.ft.com/content/e7e53c72-538c-11e8-b3ee-41e0209208ec.

Nuclear Threat Initiative (NTI). "Iran: Nuclear," June 2020. https://www.nti.org/learn/countries/iran/nuclear/.

Oskar Klevnas, Per. "Sanctions and the 'Moral Case' for War." *Global Policy Forum*, March 4, 2003. https://www.globalpolicy.org/component/content/article/170/41948.html.

Peksen, Dursun. "Better or Worse? The Effect of Economic Sanctions on Human Rights." *Journal of Peace Research* 46, no. 1 (2009): 59-77.

———. "When Do Imposed Economic Sanctions Work? A Critical Review of the Sanctions Effectiveness Literature." *Defence and Peace Economics* 30, no. 6 (September 19, 2019): 635-47. https://doi.org/10.1080/10242694.2019.1625250.

Piovesan, Flavia. "Social, Economic and Cultural Rights and Civil and Political Rights." *Sur—International Journal on Human Rights*, August 10, 2017. https://sur.conectas.org/en/social-economic-cultural-rights-civil-political-rights/.

Riedel, Bruce. "How the Iran-Iraq War Shaped the Trajectories of Figures like Qassem Soleimani." Brookings (blog), January 9, 2020. https://www.brookings.edu/blog/order-from-chaos/2020/01/09/how-the-iran-iraq-war-shaped-the-trajectories-of-figures-like-qassem-soleimani/.

Saunders, Paul J. "When Sanctions Lead to War." *The New York Times*, August 21, 2014, sec. Opinion. https://www.nytimes.com/2014/08/22/opinion/when-sanctions-lead-to-war.html.

Shahidsaless, Shahir. "For Iran, Retaliation Is More than a Matter of Saving Face." *Middle East Eye*, January 8, 2020. http://www.middleeasteye.net/opinion/how-will-iran-retaliate-against-us-soleimanis-assassination.

Slavin, Barbara. "Majority of Iranians Now Want to Quit Nuclear Deal." *Al-Monitor*, October 16, 2019. https://www.al-monitor.com/pulse/originals/2019/10/iran-poll-majority-exit-nuclear-deal-jcpoa.html.

Smeets, Maarten. "Can Economic Sanctions Be Effective? (Working Paper)." World Trade Organization, March 15, 2018, 19.

Smith, Dan. "The US Withdrawal from the Iran Deal: One Year On." Stockholm International Peace Research Institute (SIPRI), May 7, 2019. https://www.sipri.org/commentary/expert-comment/2019/us-withdrawal-iran-deal-one-year.

State Secretariat for Economic Affairs (SECO). "Smart Sanctions—Targeted Sanctions," March 24, 2017. https://www.seco.admin.ch/seco/en/home/Aussenwirtschafts-politik_Wirtschaftliche_Zusammenarbeit/Wirtschaftsbeziehungen/exportkontrollen-und-sanktionen/sanktionen-embargos/smart-sanctions--gezielte-sanktionen.html.

Stratfor Worldview. "Iran May up Its Aggression As the U.S. Expands Sanctions." *RealClear Defense*, November 5, 2019. https://www.realcleardefense.com/articles/2019/11/05/iran_may_up_its_aggression_as_the_us_expands_sanctions_114831-full.html.

Tabatabai, Ariane, and Annie Tracy Samuel. "Understanding the Iran Nuclear Deal through the Lens of the Iran-Iraq War." *Lawfare*, July 16, 2017. https://www.lawfareblog.com/understanding-iran-nuclear-deal-through-lens-iran-iraq-war.

The White House—President Barack Obama. "The Historic Deal That Will Prevent Iran from Acquiring a Nuclear Weapon." Accessed October 21, 2020. https://obamawhitehouse.archives.gov/issues/foreign-policy/iran-deal.

Tostensen, Arne, and Beate Bull. "Are Smart Sanctions Feasible?" *World Politics* 54, no. 3 (April 2002): 373-403. https://doi.org/10.1353/wp.2002.0010.

United Nations Human Rights Office of the High Commissioner (OHCHR). "Key Concepts on ESCRs—Are Economic, Social and Cultural Rights Fundamentally Different from Civil and Political Rights?" Accessed October 21, 2020.

https://www.ohchr.org/EN/Issues/ESCR/Pages/AreESCRfun-damentallydifferentfromcivilandpoliticalrights.aspx.

U.S. Embassy in Georgia. "Iran Sanctions/Europe in on-Record Briefing by Special Representative for Iran Brian Hook (November 2)," November 2, 2018. https://ge.usembassy.gov/iran-sanctions-europe-in-on-record-briefing-by-special-representative-for-iran-brian-hook-november-2/.

Vaez, Ali. "Missing the Point on Iran's Nuclear Breakout Time." *The International Crisis Group*, March 2, 2015. https://www.crisisgroup.org/middle-east-north-africa/gulf-and-arabian-peninsula/iran/missing-point-iran-s-nuclear-breakout-time.

Van Nederveen, Gilles. "Do Sanctions Lead to War?" *Foreign Policy Journal*, January 7, 2012. https://www.foreignpolicyjournal.com/2012/01/07/do-sanctions-lead-to-war/.

Winter, Chase. "What Is the EU-Iran Payment Vehicle INSTEX?" DW.COM. Accessed October 21, 2020. https://www.dw.com/en/what-is-the-eu-iran-payment-vehicle-instex/a-47306401.

White House, The. "Background Press Call on Iran Sanctions," January 12, 2018. https://www.whitehouse.gov/briefings-statements/background-press-call-iran-sanctions/.

Chapter 3: Effects of Sanctions

"A Growing Crisis: The Impact of Sanctions and Regime Policies on Iranians' Economic and Social Rights." International Campaign for Human Rights in Iran, 2013. https://www.iranhumanrights.org/wp-content/uploads/A-Growing-Crisis.pdf.

Alavi, Ahmad. "Iran's Official Figures Indicate Alarming Unemployment Rate Later This Year." Radio Farda. January

9, 2019. https://en.radiofarda.com/a/iran-official-figures-alarming-unemployment-2019/29698225.html.

Al Jazeera. "Timeline: Sanctions on Iran." October 17, 2012. https://www.aljazeera.com/economy/2012/10/17/timeline-sanctions-on-iran.

Azarnoush, Shora. "Iran's Economy Plummets under Weight of Sanctions." DW.COM, October 23, 2019. https://www.dw.com/en/irans-economy-plummets-under-weight-of-sanctions/a-50950471.

Batmanghelidj, Esfandyar. "Tougher U.S. Sanctions Will Enrich Iran's Revolutionary Guards." *Foreign Policy*, October 4, 2018. https://foreignpolicy.com/2018/10/04/irans-revolutionary-guard-corps-wont-suffer-from-stronger-u-s-sanctions-they-ll-benefit-irgc-trump-sanctions/.

BBC News. "Six Charts That Show How Hard US Sanctions Have Hit Iran," December 9, 2019. https://www.bbc.com/news/world-middle-east-48119109.

Benjamin, Medea, and Sussan Tahmasebi. "Iranian Women Squeezed By US Sanctions, COVID-19 and Their Government." *Common Dreams*, May 14, 2020. https://www.commondreams.org/views/2020/05/14/iranian-women-squeezed-us-sanctions-covid-19-and-their-government.

Csicsmann, László. "Struggling for a Sustainable Economy: Iran after the JCPOA." MENARA Future Notes No. 19, March 2019. http://www.cidob.org/en/publications/publication_series/menara_papers/future_notes/struggling_for_a_sustainable_economy_iran_after_the_jcpoa.

Dizaji, Sajjad Faraji. "The Effects of Oil Shocks on Government Expenditures and Government Revenues Nexus (with an Application to Iran's Sanctions)." *Economic Modelling* 40, no. C (2014): 299-313.

Erdbrink, Thomas. "Already Plagued by Inflation, Iran Is Bracing for Worse." *The New York Times*, July 1, 2012, sec. World. https://www.nytimes.com/2012/07/02/world/middleeast/inflation-plagued-iran-prepares-for-worse.html.

———. "Iran's Economic Crisis Drags Down the Middle Class Almost Overnight (Published 2018)." *The New York Times*, December 26, 2018, sec. World. https://www.nytimes.com/2018/12/26/world/middleeast/iran-middle-class-currency-inflation.html.

Gharagozlou, Leila. "Inflation Runs Rampant in Tehran as Iran's Government Struggles to Stem Rising Food Prices." CNBC, July 17, 2019. https://www.cnbc.com/2019/07/17/inflation-rampant-in-tehran-as-iran-struggles-to-stem-rising-food-prices.html.

Horri, Mahin. "Why Iran's Workers Are Constantly Protesting to Delayed Payments." People's Mojahedin Organization of Iran (PMOI), August 27, 2019. https://english.mojahedin.org/i/iran-workers-unpaid-wages-labor-protests.

"Iran Economic Monitor: Weathering Economic Challenges." World Bank Group, Fall 2018. http://documents1.worldbank.org/curated/en/676781543436287317/pdf/Iran-Economic-Monitor-Weathering-Economic-Challenges.pdf.

Kalhor, Navid. "Why Iran Could Be Approaching Hyperinflation in Coming Years." Al-Monitor, August 9, 2020. https://www.al-monitor.com/pulse/originals/2020/08/iran-economy-currency-rial-hyperinflation-stock-exchange.html.

Khatinoglu, Dalga. "Government Debt, Deficit, Money Supply Soar, Iran Central Bank Reveals." Radio Farda, February 14, 2020. https://en.radiofarda.com/a/government-debt-deficit-money-supply-soar-iran-central-bank-reveals/30434199.html.

Laub, Zachary, and Kali Robinson. "What Is the Status of the Iran Nuclear Agreement?" Council on Foreign Relations, January 7, 2020.

https://www.cfr.org/backgrounder/what-status-iran-nuclear-agreement.

Mohseni-Cheraghlou, Amin. "Unemployment Crisis in Iraq and Iran: A Chronic Dilemma for State and Society." *Gulf International Forum* (blog), March 3, 2020. https://gulfif.org/unemployment-crisis-in-iraq-and-iran-a-chronic-dilemma-for-state-and-society/.

Radio Farda. "Iran's Statistical Center Reports 7.6 Percent Decline in GDP," February 10, 2020. https://en.radiofarda.com/a/iran-s-statistical-center-reports-7-6-percent-decline-in-gdp/30427214.html.

Shahidsaless, Shahir. "An Unstable Iran Would Actually Be Very Bad for the US." Middle East Eye, August 30, 2018. http://www.middleeasteye.net/opinion/unstable-iran-would-actually-be-very-bad-us.

Sharafedin, Bozorgmehr. "Iranian Jobs Go as U.S. Sanctions Start to Bite." *Reuters*, November 19, 2018. https://www.reuters.com/article/us-usa-iran-sanctions-jobs-idUSKCN1NO14C.

Studer, Elisabeth. "L'Iran demande à ses constructeurs de produire des pièces PSA." *Leblogauto.com* (blog), August 29, 2019. https://www.leblogauto.com/2019/08/iran-constructeurs-nationaux-auto-production-pieces-psa.html.

Tharoor, Ishaan. "Sanctions on Iran Cost the U.S. as Much as $175 Billion, Study Says." *Washington Post*, July 16, 2014. https://www.washingtonpost.com/news/worldviews/wp/2014/07/16/sanctions-on-iran-cost-the-u-s-as-much-as-175-billion-study-says/.

The White House. "President Donald J. Trump Is Working to Bring Iran's Oil Exports to Zero," April 22, 2019. https://www.whitehouse.gov/briefings-statements/president-donald-j-trump-working-bring-irans-oil-exports-zero/.

World Bank. "GDP Growth (Annual %)—Iran, Islamic Rep. |
Data." Accessed October 21, 2020. https://data.worldbank.org/
indicator/NY.GDP.MKTP.KD.ZG?locations=IR.

World Bank. "Iran's Economic Update—October 2019," October 9,
2019. https://www.worldbank.org/en/country/iran/publication/
economic-update-october-2019.

"World Economic Outlook: Global Manufacturing Downturn,
Rising Trade Barriers." Washington, DC: International
Monetary Fund, October 2019. https://www.imf.org/~/media/
Files/Publications/WEO/2019/October/English/text.ashx.

Zahedi, Razieh, and Pooya Azadi. "Central Banking in Iran." *Stanford University*, Stanford Iran 2040 Project, no. Working Paper
No. 5 (June 2018): 38.

Chapter 4: Health

Azodi, Sina. "How US Sanctions Hinder Iranians' Access to Medicine." *Atlantic Council* (blog), May 31, 2019.
https://www.atlanticcouncil.org/blogs/iransource/how-us-sanctions-hinder-iranians-access-to-medicne/.

Basravi, Zein. "Iran's Wealth Gap: Tens of Millions Struggle to Get
By." *Al Jazeera*, January 20, 2018. https://www.aljazeera.com/
videos/2018/01/20/irans-wealth-gap-tens-of-millions-struggle-to-get-by/.

Champion, Marc, and Golnar Motevalli. "How Iran's Virus Fight
Is Tied to Struggle With U.S." *Bloomberg*, August 3, 2020.
https://www.bloomberg.com/news/articles/2020-06-14/how-iran-s-virus-fight-is-tied-to-struggle-with-u-s-quicktake.

Dehghan, Saeed Kamali. "Haemophiliac Iranian Boy 'Dies after
Sanctions Disrupt Medicine Supplies.'" *The Guardian*, November 14, 2012, sec. World news.

https://www.theguardian.com/world/2012/nov/14/sanctions-stop-medicines-reaching-sick-iranians.

Gorji, A. "Sanctions against Iran: The Impact on Health Services." *Iranian Journal of Public Health* 43, no. 3 (March 2014): 381-82.

Human Rights Watch. "'Maximum Pressure': US Economic Sanctions Harm Iranians' Right to Health," October 29, 2019. https://www.hrw.org/report/2019/10/29/maximum-pressure/us-economic-sanctions-harm-iranians-right-health.

"Iran Healthcare Sector Analysis 2016-2021—Research and Markets." *India Pharma News.* August 23, 2016. http://global.factiva.com/redir/default.aspx?P=sa&an=AT-PHAM0020160824ec8n000e5&cat=a&ep=ASE.

Kokabisaghi, Fatemeh. "Assessment of the Effects of Economic Sanctions on Iranians' Right to Health by Using Human Rights Impact Assessment Tool: A Systematic Review." *International Journal of Health Policy and Management* 7, no. 5 (January 20, 2018): 374-93. https://doi.org/10.15171/ijhpm.2017.147.

Mahjoub, Nikki. "Iranian 'hungry' babies waiting for powdered milk." BBC Persian. British Broadcasting Corporation, October 30, 2012. https://doi.org/10/121030_l21_infant_formula_health_sanction.shtml.

Mohammadi, Dara. "US-Led Economic Sanctions Strangle Iran's Drug Supply." *The Lancet* 381, no. 9863 (January 26, 2013): 279. https://doi.org/10.1016/S0140-6736(13)60116-6.

Murphy, Adrianna, Zhaleh Abdi, Iraj Harirchi, Martin McKee, and Elham Ahmadnezhad. "Economic Sanctions and Iran's Capacity to Respond to COVID-19." *The Lancet Public Health* 5, no. 5 (May 2020): e254. https://doi.org/10.1016/S2468-2667(20)30083-9.

Murphy, Christopher S., and et al., March 26, 2020. https://www.murphy.senate.gov/imo/media/doc/Final%20Sanctions%20Letter%20w%20Sigs.pdf.

Namazi, Siamak. "Sanctions and Medical Supply Shortages in Iran." *Wilson Center*, Viewpoints No. 20, February 2013, 12.

Paddock, Catharine. "Hemophilia Cure? Gene Therapy Trial Shows Dramatic Results." *Medical News Today*, December 15, 2017. https://www.medicalnewstoday.com/articles/320382.

Refugees, United Nations High Commissioner for. "Situation of Human Rights in the Islamic Republic of Iran : Note / by the Secretary-General." Refworld, October 4, 2013. https://www.refworld.org/docid/534e4e424.html.

Reuters Editorial. "Iran Rejects U.S. Offer of Coronavirus Help." *Reuters*, August 26, 2020. https://www.reuters.com/video/watch/idPsP9?now=true.

Sadjadpour, Karim. "Iran's Coronavirus Disaster." Carnegie Endowment for International Peace, March 25, 2020. https://carnegieendowment.org/2020/03/25/iran-s-coronavirus-disaster-pub-81367.

Saul, Jonathan, Ana Mano, and Joori Roh. "Iran Struggles to Buy Food in a World Wary of Touching Its Money." *Reuters*, July 30, 2020. https://www.reuters.com/article/us-iran-food-imports-insight-idUSKCN24V0NO.

Setayesh, Sogol, and Tim K. Mackey. "Addressing the Impact of Economic Sanctions on Iranian Drug Shortages in the Joint Comprehensive Plan of Action: Promoting Access to Medicines and Health Diplomacy." *Globalization and Health* 12, no. 1 (June 8, 2016): 31. https://doi.org/10.1186/s12992-016-0168-6.

Smyth, Gareth. "How a Misleading Report on Iran from a Hawkish 'think Tank' Made Its Way to Trump Administration Talking Points." *Responsible Statecraft* (blog), April 22, 2020. https://responsiblestatecraft.org/2020/04/22/how-a-misleading-report-on-iran-from-a-fdd-trump-administration-talking-points/.

Talley, Ian, and Benoit Faucon. "U.S. to Block Iran's Request to IMF for $5 Billion Loan to Fight Coronavirus." *Wall Street Journal*, April 7, 2020, sec. World. https://www.wsj.com/articles/u-s-to-block-irans-request-to-imf-for-5-billion-loan-to-fight-coronavirus-11586301732.

United States Institue of Peace: The Iran Primer. "Dozens of Countries Send COVID-19 Aid to Iran," April 29, 2020. https://iranprimer.usip.org/blog/2020/apr/07/dozens-countries-send-covid-19-aid-iran.

U.S. Department of the Treasury. "United States Announces Successful Initial Transactions Through Humanitarian Channel for Iran," January 30, 2020. https://home.treasury.gov/news/press-releases/sm890.

Worldometer. "Coronavirus Update (Live)," October 22, 2020. https://www.worldometers.info/coronavirus/?utm_campaign=homeAdvegas1?%22%20%5Cl%22countries.

Chapter 5: Food

Bourse & Bazaar. "Iranians Forced to Forgo Meat Staples as Prices Soar." May 9, 2019. https://www.bourseandbazaar.com/articles/2019/5/8/iranians-forced-to-forgo-meat-staples-as-price-soar.

Bozorgmehr, Najmeh. "Iran Warned on Food Security." *Financial Times*, April 3, 2013. https://www.ft.com/content/809b63da-8fb9-11e2-9239-00144feabdco.

Bozorgmehr, Najmeh, and Monavar Khalaj. "Poor Iranians Bear Brunt of Sanctions as Food Prices Soar." *Financial Times*, August 6, 2018. https://www.ft.com/content/doe17cac-94dc-11e8-b747-fb1e803ee64e.

Crabtree, Steve. "Half of Iranians Lack Adequate Money for Food, Shelter." Gallup, July 1, 2013. https://news.gallup.com/

poll/163295/half-iranians-lack-adequate-money-food-shelter.
aspx.

Dehghan, Saeed Kamali. "Iranian Baby Milk Shortage Blamed on
Sanctions." *The Guardian*, November 6, 2012, sec. World news.
https://www.theguardian.com/world/iran-blog/2012/nov/06/
baby-milk-shortage-iran-sanctions.

Demers, Jayson. "Small Business Growth Has Stalled and That's Bad
for All of Us." *Time*, March 23, 2017. https://time.com/4709959/
small-business-growth/.

Erdbrink, Thomas. "Iran Capitalizing on a Taste for America's Biggest Brands (Published 2015)." *The New York Times*, August 2,
2015, sec. World. https://www.nytimes.com/2015/08/03/world/
middleeast/a-burger-joint-thats-irans-answer-to-mcdonalds.
html.

Explore Parts Unknown. "Iran." Accessed October 22, 2020.
https://explorepartsunknown.com/destination/iran/.

Gambrell, Jon. "Some Iranians Embrace American Culture with
a Coke and a Smile." *Christian Science Monitor*, July 11, 2019.
https://www.csmonitor.com/World/Middle-East/2019/0711/
Some-Iranians-embrace-American-culture-with-a-Coke-and-
a-smile.

Global Nutrition Report. "Iran (Islamic Republic of) Nutrition
Profile." Accessed October 22, 2020.
https://globalnutritionreport.org/resources/nutrition-profiles/
asia/southern-asia/iran-islamic-republic/.

Gordon, C Joy. "Crippling Iran: The UN Security Council and
the Tactic of Deliberate Ambiguity." *Georgetown Journal of
International Law* 44, no. 3 (2013): 973-1006.

Heslot, Soazic. "Iran's Food Security." *Future Directions International*
(blog), August 8, 2014. https://www.futuredirections.org.au/
publication/iran-s-food-security/.

Homa. "TAHCHIN MORGH ته چی نی مرغ." Persian Mamma, October 6, 2015. https://persianmama.com/tahchin-morgh/.

IFP Editorial Staff. "Iran Producing $80 Billion Worth of Agricultural Products." *Iran Front Page* (blog), October 23, 2019. https://ifpnews.com/iran-producing-80-billion-worth-of-agricultural-products.

McDowell, Erin, and Hillary Hoffower. "Here's the Income It Takes for a Family of 4 to Be Considered Poor in Every State." Business Insider, November 1, 2019. https://www.businessinsider.com/income-amount-poverty-level-in-every-state-2018-11.

Mehran, Azita. "Turmeric & Saffron: Dopiazeh Aloo." *Turmeric & Saffron* (blog), July 10, 2018. https://turmericsaffron.blogspot.com/2018/07/dopiazeh-aloo.html.

———. "Turmeric & Saffron: Javaher Polow—Persian Jeweled Rice." *Turmeric & Saffron* (blog), January 10, 2011. https://turmericsaffron.blogspot.com/2011/01/javaher-polow-persian-jeweled-rice.html.

———. "Turmeric & Saffron: Mirza Ghasemi." *Turmeric & Saffron* (blog), February 11, 2009. https://turmericsaffron.blogspot.com/2009/02/mirza-ghasemi-northern-irans-eggplants.html.

Michel, David. "Iran's Troubled Quest for Food Self-Sufficiency." *Atlantic Council* (blog), July 9, 2019. https://www.atlanticcouncil.org/blogs/iransource/iran-s-troubled-quest-for-food-self-sufficiency/.

Mostaghim, Ramin, and Melissa Etehad. "Middle-Class Iranians Resort to Buying Rotting Produce as U.S. Sanctions Take Toll." *Los Angeles Times*, August 28, 2019, sec. World & Nation. https://www.latimes.com/world-nation/story/2019-08-27/iran-trump-sanctions-economy-food-medicine-shortage.

Pishbin, Shaahin. "The Best Fast Food Spots In Tehran." *Culture Trip*, September 27, 2016. https://theculturetrip.com/middle-east/iran/articles/the-5-best-fast-food-spots-in-tehran-from-burgers-to-falafel/.

Price, Massoume. "Persian Cuisine, a Brief History." Culture of Iran, October 2009. http://www.cultureofiran.com/persian_cuisine.html.

Radio Farda. "As Cost Of Living Rises In Iran Millions Fall Under Poverty Line." Radio Farda, June 5, 2020. https://en.radiofarda.com/a/cost-of-living-rises-in-iran-millions-fall-under-poverty-line/30654495.html.

Radio Farda. "Food Price Inflation In Iran At 30 Percent According To Latest Report," Radio Farda, January 20, 2020. https://en.radiofarda.com/a/food-price-inflation-in-iran-at-30-percent-according-to-latest-report/30387564.html.

Refugees, United Nations High Commissioner for. "Situation of Human Rights in the Islamic Republic of Iran : Note / by the Secretary-General." Refworld, October 4, 2013. https://www.refworld.org/docid/534e4e424.html.

Saul, Jonathan, and Parisa Hafezi. "Exclusive: Global Traders Halt New Iran Food Deals as U.S. Sanctions Bite—Sources." *Reuters*, December 21, 2018. https://www.reuters.com/article/us-iran-nuclear-food-exclusive-idUSKCN1OK1OR.

Sedghi, Sarra. "How Bootleg Fast Food Conquered Iran." Atlas Obscura, March 29, 2018. http://www.atlasobscura.com/articles/fast-food-in-iran.

Shafia, Louisa. "Persian Food Primer: 10 Essential Iranian Dishes." *Food Republic* (blog), October 29, 2014. https://www.foodrepublic.com/2014/10/29/persian-food-primer-10-essential-iranian-dishes/.

Shams, Anahita. "Does Shiraz Wine Come from Iran?" *BBC News*, February 3, 2017, sec. Middle East. https://www.bbc.com/news/world-middle-east-38771806.

Tehran Times. "65% of Iranian Population Overweight, Obese." December 23, 2018. https://www.tehrantimes.com/news/431000/65-of-Iranian-population-overweight-obese.

Tehran Times. "'Childhood Obesity Rate Worryingly Soars in Iran,'" March 16, 2019. https://www.tehrantimes.com/news/434135/Childhood-obesity-rate-worryingly-soars-in-Iran.

Chapter 6: Environment

Angwin, Richard. "Dust Storms—a Modern Plague on Iran." *Al Jazeera*, June 4, 2014. https://www.aljazeera.com/news/2014/6/4/dust-storms-a-modern-plague-on-iran.

Badawi, Tamer. "Iran's Water Problem." Carnegie Endowment for International Peace, December 11, 2018. https://carnegieendowment.org/sada/77935.

Baker, Aryn. "A Side Effect of Iranian Sanctions: Tehran's Bad Air." *Time*, July 7, 2014. https://time.com/2986299/iranian-sanctions-create-tehran-air-pollution/.

Balikhani, Vida. "Poor Quality Gasoline Deadly for Iranians." *Atlantic Council* (blog), February 16, 2017. https://www.atlanticcouncil.org/blogs/iransource/poor-quality-gasoline-deadly-for-iranians/.

Bodetti, Austin. "Iran Struggles With Food Security Amid Sanctions." LobeLog, September 16, 2019. https://lobelog.com/iran-struggles-with-food-security-amid-sanctions/.

Brown, Jessica. "Cloud Seeding: Should We Be Playing God and Controlling the Weather?" *The Independent*, January 17, 2018. https://www.independent.co.uk/news/long_reads/cloud-seeding-weather-control-manipulate-effects-chemicals-climate-change-a8160146.html.

Dilleen, Connor. "Will Renewed US Sanctions Worsen Iran's Water Security Crisis?" The Strategist—The Australian Strategic Policy

Institute (ASPI), August 7, 2018. https://www.aspistrategist.org.au/
will-renewed-us-sanctions-worsen-irans-water-security-crisis/.

Doucet, Lyse. "Nuclear Deal Could Give Iran Technologies to Cut
Pollution." *BBC News*, November 30, 2015, sec. Asia.
https://www.bbc.com/news/world-asia-34965973.

Eghtesad Online. "Iran Water Industry Counting the Cost of US
Sanctions," October 6, 2019. https://www.en.eghtesadonline.
com/Section-economy-4/30446-iran-water-industry-counting-
the-cost-of-us-sanctions.

Encyclopedia Britannica. "Qanāt." Accessed October 22, 2020.
https://www.britannica.com/technology/qanat.

Erdbrink, Thomas. "Scarred Riverbeds and Dead Pistachio Trees
in a Parched Iran." *The New York Times*, December 18, 2015, sec.
World. https://www.nytimes.com/2015/12/19/world/middleeast/
scarred-riverbeds-and-dead-pistachio-trees-in-a-parched-iran.
html.

———. "Video: The Empty River of Life." *The New York Times*,
May 5, 2015, sec. World. https://www.nytimes.com/video/
world/100000003582033/the-empty-river-of-live.html.

Gang, Ding. "Self-Sufficiency Helps Iran Counter Sanctions."
Global Times, May 15, 2019. https://www.globaltimes.cn/
content/1150016.shtml.

Hamidi, Fardine, trans. "Iran's Zagros Mountains Face Water
Shortage, Threatening Wildlife, Plants." Khayan Life, February 24, 2019. https://kayhanlife.com/society/environment/
irans-zagros-mountains-face-water-shortage-threatening-
wildlife-plants/.

"Hamoun Wetlands: Current Situation and the Way Forward."
United Nations Development Program (UNDP), March
2014. https://www.undp.org/content/dam/iran/docs/News/
2014/March%202014/Towards%20a%20solution%20for%20

Iran's%20dying%20wetlands/Hamoun%20Wetland/Hamoun
%20Info%20Sheet.pdf.

ICR Independent Evaluation Group. "IEG: ICR Review." World
Bank Group, April 29, 2014. http://documents1.worldbank.org/
curated/en/127941474564344139/pdf/000020051-20140626110127.
pdf.

Karami, Arash. "Khamenei Says Iran Must Go Green." *Al-Monitor*, November 18, 2015. https://www.al-monitor.com/pulse/
originals/2015/11/iran-green-climate-change-khamenei.html.

Khalatbari, L., J. C. Brito, A. Ghoddousi, H. Abolghasemi, U. Breitenmoser, Ch Breitenmoser-Würsten, G. H. Yusefi, S. Ostrowski,
and S. M. Durant. "Sanctioning to Extinction in Iran." *Science*
362, no. 6420 (December 14, 2018): 1255-1255.
https://doi.org/10.1126/science.aav8221.

Lewis, Tom, and Kaveh Madani. "End of Sanctions May Help Iran
Face an Accelerating Environmental Crisis." *The Guardian*,
January 20, 2016, sec. World news.
https://www.theguardian.com/world/iran-blog/2016/jan/20/
iran-end-of-sanctions-prompt-environmental-crisis.

Mehdi, Syed Zafar. "US Sanctions Cause Environmental Crisis in
Iran." Anadolu Agency (AA), December 20, 2019.
https://www.aa.com.tr/en/middle-east/us-sanctions-cause-
environmental-crisis-in-iran/1679080.

Mesgaran, Mohsen B., Kaveh Madani, Hossein Hashemi, and
Pooya Azadi. "Iran's Land Suitability for Agriculture." *Scientific Reports* 7, no. 1 (August 9, 2017): 7670.
https://doi.org/10.1038/s41598-017-08066-y.

Michel, David. "Iran's Impending Water Crisis," 2017.

Mostatabi, Mana. "Sanctioning Iran's Climate." *Atlantic Council* (blog), May 1, 2019. https://www.atlanticcouncil.org/blogs/
menasource/sanctioning-iran-s-climate/.

NASA Earth Observatory. "Desert." NASA Earth Observatory, October 22, 2020. https://earthobservatory.nasa.gov/biome/biodesert.php.

Radio Farda. "Harmful Oil Bi-Product Used In Iranian Cities, Polluting The Air," January 19, 2020. https://en.radiofarda.com/a/harmful-oil-bi-product-used-in-iranian-cities-polluting-the-air/30385903.html.

Radio Farda. "Residents Abandoning Regions With Increasingly Fierce Sandstorms," April 30, 2018. https://en.radiofarda.com/a/residents-abandoning-regions-with-increasingly-fierce-sandstorms/29200612.html.

Reuters Staff. "South Korea's Hyundai E&C Cancels $521 Million Petrochemicals Deal, Cites Iran Financing Failure." *Reuters*, October 29, 2018. https://www.reuters.com/article/us-hyundaie-c-iran-idUSKCN1N30U9.

Ritter, Kayla. "Tehran Faces Crisis As Iran's Water Supply Runs Low." *Circle of Blue* (blog), June 6, 2018. https://www.circleofblue.org/2018/middle-east/tehran-faces-crisis-as-irans-water-supply-runs-low/.

Roche, María Yetano, Cordelia Paetz, and Carmen Dienst. "Implementation of Nationally Determined Contributions—Islamic Republic of Iran." *Umwelt Bundesamt*, 2018, 42.

Saatsaz, Masoud. *A Historical Investigation on Water Resources Management in Iran*, 2019. https://www.researchgate.net/publication/330522060_A_Historical_Investigation_on_Water_Resources_Management_in_Iran.

Sengupta, Somini. "Warming, Water Crisis, Then Unrest: How Iran Fits an Alarming Pattern." *The New York Times*, January 18, 2018, sec. Climate. https://www.nytimes.com/2018/01/18/climate/water-iran.html.

Sharafedin, Bozorgmehr. "Iran's Thirsty Energy Industry Runs up against Water Shortage." *Reuters*, October 29, 2019. https://

www.reuters.com/article/us-iran-energy-water-analysis-idUSKBN1X80H5.

Tehran Times. "Iran Proposes Inclusion of Water-Related Issues in COP 24," November 22, 2017. https://www.tehrantimes.com/news/418658/Iran-proposes-inclusion-of-water-related-issues-in-COP-24.

Tehran Times. "150 Animals in Danger of Extinction in Iran." April 13, 2019. https://www.tehrantimes.com/news/434593/150-animals-in-danger-of-extinction-in-Iran.

The Royal Danish Embassy in Tehran. "The Agriculture and Food Market in Iran." Danish Agriculture & Food Council, March 2017. https://lf.dk/~/media/lf/for-medlemmer/virksomhedsmedlem-hos-os/ingrediensnyhedsbrev/2017/april17/report-the-agriculture-and-food-market-in-iran-.pdf?la=da.

The Korea Herald. "Daelim Revokes W2tln Deal with Iranian Oil Company in Wake," June 1, 2018. http://www.koreaherald.com/view.php?ud=20180601000862.

UNESCO World Heritage Centre. "The Persian Qanat." UNESCO World Heritage Centre. Accessed October 22, 2020. https://whc.unesco.org/en/list/1506/.

Walker. "Hitting Nature Where It Hurts: Iran Feels the Pernicious Effects of US Sanctions on Biodiversity Conservation." Equal Times, February 27, 2019. https://www.equaltimes.org/hitting-nature-where-it-hurts-iran.

Worldometer. "Largest Countries in the World by Area." Accessed October 22, 2020. https://www.worldometers.info/geography/largest-countries-in-the-world/.

Chapter 7: Housing

Bizaer, Maysam. "Iranians Struggle to Afford Housing as Prices Soar." Al Jazeera, August 5, 2019. https://www.aljazeera.com/

economy/2019/8/5/iranians-struggle-to-afford-housing-as-prices-soar.

Fanni, Zohreh. "Cities and Urbanization in Iran after the Islamic Revolution." *Cities* 23 (December 1, 2006): 407-11. https://doi.org/10.1016/j.cities.2006.08.003.

Hulpachova, Marketa. "Iran's Economy Struggles to Support Ahmadinejad's Ill-Conceived Housing Vision." *The Guardian*, January 30, 2014, sec. World news. https://www.theguardian.com/world/iran-blog/2014/jan/30/irans-economy-struggles-to-support-ahmadinejads-ill-conceived-housing-vision.

Katiraie, Jubin. "The Nightmare of Rising Prices and Housing Rent in Iran." *Iran Focus* (blog), June 22, 2020. https://www.iranfocus.com/en/economy/34589-the-nightmare-of-rising-prices-and-housing-rent-in-iran/.

Khajehpour, Bijan. "Iran's Housing Crisis." Al-Monitor, June 17, 2013. https://www.al-monitor.com/pulse/originals/2013/06/iran-housing-sector.html.

Khalaj, Monavar. "Impoverished Iranians Forced to Leave Tehran for a Cheaper Life." *Financial Times*, September 29, 2019. https://www.ft.com/content/4a6b53ee-df60-11e9-9743-db5a370481bc.

———. "Sanction End to Help Iran Property Market." *Financial Times*, September 15, 2015. https://www.ft.com/content/1560d-da0-4657-11e5-af2f-4d6e0e5eda22.

Laub, Karin, and Mohammad Nasiri. "US Sanctions Squeeze Iran Middle Class, Upend Housing Sector." *AP News*, July 23, 2019. https://apnews.com/article/f163a13259704e68aeb2197dc1afed81.

Nima, Adele. "26 Million Denied Homes as Iran's Housing Market Prices Jump by 90%." *Iran News Wire* (blog), June 25, 2019. https://irannewswire.org/26-million-denied-homes-as-irans-housing-market-prices-jump-by-90/.

Parviz, Salman. "Despite Economic Fallout Tehran Real Estate Market Flourishes." Tehran Times, June 30, 2020. https://www.tehrantimes.com/news/449417/Despite-economic-fallout-Tehran-real-estate-market-flourishes.

Correspondent, Tehran Bureau. "Tehran Landlords and Tenants Lock Horns in Heat of Property Boom." *The Guardian*, February 5, 2013, sec. World news. https://www.theguardian.com/world/blog/2013/feb/05/tehran-landlord-tenant-property-boom.

Rasanah Editorial Team. "25 Square Meter Apartments: The Contradiction between Iran's New Housing Policy and Its Official Population Policy." *Rasanah International Institute for Iranian Studies* (blog), August 5, 2020. https://rasanah-iiis.org/english/monitoring-and-translation/reports/25-square-meter-apartments-the-contradiction-between-irans-new-housing-policy-and-its-official-population-policy/.

VOA News. "Fear of Bubble as Sanctions Stoke Iran Property Boom," May 8, 2013. https://www.voanews.com/world-news/middle-east-dont-use/fear-bubble-sanctions-stoke-iran-property-boom.

Tehran Times. "1st Phase of National Housing Action Plan Completed in Southern Iran," May 30, 2020. https://www.tehrantimes.com/news/448356/1st-phase-of-National-Housing-Action-Plan-completed-in-southern.

Wright, Robin. "Ghost Towers: The View from Iran's Housing Crisis." *The New Yorker*. Accessed October 22, 2020. https://www.newyorker.com/magazine/2019/10/21/ghost-towers.

Zanjani, Habibollah. "Housing in Iran." *Encyclopaedia Iranica*, March 23, 2012. https://iranicaonline.org/articles/housing-in-iran.

Chapter 8: Education

Bezhan, Frud. "Class Act: Iranian Campaign to Allow Afghan Refugee Kids Into School." *Radio Free Europe / Radio Liberty.* September 02, 2017. https://www.rferl.org/a/iran-afghanistan-refugee-children-school-access-policies-campaign/28712296.html.

Bhoyroo, Farha. "Afghan children learn side by side with Iranian peers." *UNHCR. The UN Refugee Agency.* 10 December 2019. https://www.unhcr.org/news/briefing/2019/12/5dea18ac4/support-needed-refugee-education-iran.html.

Butler, Declan. "How US sanctions are crippling science in Iran," *Nature news.* 24 September, 2019. https://www.nature.com/articles/d41586-019-02795-y.

Catanzaro, Michelle. "United States drop charges against two more scientists after Iran prisoner swap." *Nature.* 13 December 2019. https://www.nature.com/articles/d41586-019-03856-y.

CBC Radio. "A Legacy of Firsts: How an Iranian Mathematician Transcended Boundaries." CBC, September 23, 2019. https://www.cbc.ca/radio/ideas/a-legacy-of-firsts-how-an-iranian-mathematician-transcended-boundaries-1.5291599.

Dehghan, Saeed Kamali. "Iranian Students Blocked from UK Stem Courses Due to US Sanctions." *The Guardian*, June 26, 2014, sec. World news. https://www.theguardian.com/education/2014/jun/26/iran-students-kaplan-uk-stem-course-block-us-sanctions.

———. "Iranians Sue UK Banks over Closed Accounts, Claiming Racial Discrimination." *The Guardian*, March 28, 2014, sec. World news. https://www.theguardian.com/world/2014/mar/28/iranians-uk-banks-closed-accounts-claim-racial-discrimination.

Elmi, Zahra Mila. "Educational Attainment in Iran." Middle East Institute. January 29, 2009, accessed October 22, 2020. https://www.mei.edu/publications/educational-attainment-iran.

Encyclopedia Britannica. "Iran—Education." Accessed October 23, 2020. https://www.britannica.com/place/Iran/Education.

Guardian Staff. "Maryam Mirzakhani: 'The More I Spent Time on Maths, the More Excited I Got.'" *The Guardian*, August 13, 2014, sec. Science. https://www.theguardian.com/science/2014/aug/13/interview-maryam-mirzakhani-fields-medal-winner-mathematician.

Hampton, Caleb, and Simon Campbell. "Iranian Students Barred from US: Lost Money, Broken Dreams, No Answers." *The Guardian*, October 14, 2019, sec. US news. https://www.theguardian.com/us-news/2019/oct/14/iranian-students-barred-from-us-lost-money-broken-dreams-no-answers.

Havergal, Chris. "Iran Sets up Europe HE Partnerships after Sanctions Lifted." Times Higher Education (THE), March 1, 2016. https://www.timeshighereducation.com/news/iran-sets-europe-he-partnerships-after-sanctions-lifted.

Hazari, Samira. "What does school look like in Iran?" British Council. April 21, 2015. https://www.britishcouncil.org/voices-magazine/what-does-school-education-look-iran.

Iran HRM. "Repressive State and Low Quality of Education in Iran," September 22, 2019. https://iran-hrm.com/index.php/2019/09/22/repressive-state-and-low-quality-of-education-in-iran/.

Khoshnood, Arvin. "Poverty in Iran: A Critical Analysis." *Middle East Policy* 26, no. 1 (2019): 60-74. https://doi.org/10.1111/mepo.12400.

Kokabisaghi, Fatemeh, Andrew C Miller, Farshid R Bashar, Mahmood Salesi, Ali A K Zarchi, Abdalsamad Keramatfar, Mohammad A Pourhoseingholi, Hosein Amini, and Amir Vahedian-Azimi. "Impact of United States Political Sanctions on International Collaborations and Research in Iran." *BMJ Global Health* 4, no. 5 (September 3, 2019). https://doi.org/10.1136/bmjgh-2019-001692.

Lars Bevanger, Oslo. "Iranian Students Sue Norway over Expulsion." DW.COM, June 26, 2015. https://www.dw.com/en/iranian-students-sue-norway-over-expulsion/a-18540372.

Levin, Sam. "Cut off from Family, Unable to Travel: How US Sanctions Punish Iranian Americans." *The Guardian*, January 19, 2020, sec. US news. https://www.theguardian.com/us-news/2020/jan/19/iranian-americans-us-sanctions-iran.

Madani, Kaveh, and Khashayar Nikazmrad. "'Do-It-Yourself Sanctions Threaten Science Dialogue with Iran.'" *The Guardian*, February 23, 2015, sec. World news. https://www.theguardian.com/world/iran-blog/2015/feb/23/us-sanctions-science-iranian-students-umass.

Maxwell, Mary Jane. "Iran's 41-Year 'Brain Drain.'" *ShareAmerica* (blog), February 4, 2020. https://share.america.gov/irans-40-year-brain-drain/.

Malekzadeh, Shervin. "The new business of education in Iran." *Washington Post.* August 19, 2015, 8:00 am (EDT). https://www.washingtonpost.com/news/monkey-cage/wp/2015/08/19/the-new-business-of-education-in-iran/.

Mohseni-Cheraghilou, Amin. "Update from Iran: Iran's Over-Education Crises." *World Bank Blogs* (blog), October 6, 2017. https://blogs.worldbank.org/arabvoices/iran-education-crises.

Mojtahedi, Hamid. "Investing in Iran's Education Sector." Al Tamimi & Company, August 2016. https://www.tamimi.com/law-update-articles/investing-in-irans-education-sector/.

Mostaghim, Ramin and Melissa Etehad. "Middle-class Iranians resort to buying rotting produce as U.S. sanctions take toll." *Los Angeles Times*. August 28, 2019, 4:00 am. https://www.latimes.com/world-nation/story/2019-08-27/iran-trump-sanctions-economy-food-medicine-shortage.

Muller, Quentin. "Undocumented Afghans in Iran: Collateral damage of US sanctions." Comment. *The New Arab*. Published 7 December, 2018. https://english.alaraby.co.uk/english/comment/2018/12/6/undocumented-afghan-workers-forced-to-flee-iran.

National Iranian American Council (NIAC). "Sanctions Bar Educational Platform from Servicing Iranians," September 14, 2018. https://www.niacouncil.org/news/sanctions-bar-education-iranians/?locale=en.

UNESCO Institute of Statics. "Iran (Islamic Republic Of)," November 27, 2016. http://uis.unesco.org/en/country/ir.

Tavakol, Mohsen. "Medical Education Under Economic Sanctions in Iran." *Academic Medicine* 84, no. 10 (October 2009): 1324. https://doi.org/10.1097/ACM.0b013e3181b6552b.

Tehran Times. "Literacy Movement Organization Drafts Proposal on Compulsory Education," October 6, 2018. https://www.tehrantimes.com/news/428236/Literacy-Movement-Organization-drafts-proposal-on-compulsory.

Tehran Times. "Iran's Literacy Rate up to 97%," September 23, 2018. https://www.tehrantimes.com/news/427751/Iran-s-literacy-rate-up-to-97.

The Islamic Republic News Agency. "Iran's literacy movement wins UNESCO Confucius Prize." *The Islamic Republic News Agency*, September 9, 2018. https://en.irna.ir/news/83027232/Iran-s-literacy-movement-wins-UNESCO-Confucius-Prize.

Radio Farda. "Twenty Thousand PhD Graduates Are Unemployed In Iran," December 27, 2018. https://en.radiofarda.com/a/ thousands-phd-graduates-unemployed-in-iran/29679437.html.

WES Staff. "Education in Iran." World Education News + Reviews (WENR), February 7, 2017. https://wenr.wes.org/2017/02/ education-in-iran.

World Bank. "School Enrollment, Primary (% Net)—Middle East & North Africa, Iran, Islamic Rep." Accessed October 23, 2020. https://data.worldbank.org/indicator/SE.PRM.NENR?locations=ZQ-IR.

World Bank. "School Enrollment, Secondary (% Net)—Middle East & North Africa, Iran, Islamic Rep." Accessed October 23, 2020. https://data.worldbank.org/indicator/SE.SEC.NENR? locations=ZQ-IR.

Chapter 9: Arts

Alijani, Ershad. "Iranian label accused of organising 'un-islamic' fashion show," *The Observers, France 24,* March 13, 2019. https://observers.france24.com/en/20190313-iran-fashion-label-islamic.

Bekhrad, Joobin. "Iran's fascinating way to tell fortunes." BBC, 24 October 2018. http://www.bbc.com/travel/story/20181023-irans-fascinating-way-to-tell-fortunes.

France 24 English. *Iran: Lifting the Veil on Tehran's Cultural Life.* Youtube, 2016. https://www.youtube.com/watch?v=tDac-DnvUIs.

Gharleghi, Mehran. "How Iranian Architects Invented Ways to Stay Cool | British Council." *British Council* (blog), April 17, 2015. https://www.britishcouncil.org/voices-magazine/how-iranian-architects-invented-ways-stay-cool.

Hafez, Jahan Malek Khatun, and Obayd-e Zakani. *Faces of Love: Hafez and the Poets of Shiraz (Penguin Classics Deluxe Edition)*. Penguin, 2013.

Inskeep, Steve. "In Iran, A Poet's 700-Year-Old Verses Still Sets Hearts Aflame." *NPR*. February 12, 2016. https://www.npr.org/sections/parallels/2016/02/12/466408554/in-iran-a-poets-700-year-old-verses-still-set-hearts-aflame.

Jeffries, Stuart. "Landscapes of the Mind." *The Guardian*, April 16, 2005, sec. Film. https://www.theguardian.com/film/2005/apr/16/art.

Khalaj, Monavar. "Curtain Comes down on Iran's Theatre Boom." *Financial Times*, January 11, 2019. https://www.ft.com/content/7e778152-01ea-11e9-99df-6183d3002ee1.

New World Encyclopedia. "Hafez." Accessed October 23, 2020. https://www.newworldencyclopedia.org/entry/Hafez.

Partovi, Pouya. "O-Hum Artist Biography." All Music. Accessed October 22, 2020. https://www.allmusic.com/artist/o-hum-mn0001428284.

Pazhoohi, Farid. "Interview with Shahram Sharbaf, Frontman of O-Hum: Part I." *Mideast Tunes* (blog), December 28, 2011. https://blog.mideastunes.com/post/14936823733/interview-with-shahram-sharbaf-frontman-of-o-hum.

Proctor, Rebecca Anne. "For Years, Iran's Art Scene Has Been a Pioneer in the Mideast. Now US Sanctions Are Knocking Its Artists Back to the 18th Century." Artnet News, June 17, 2019. https://news.artnet.com/art-world/iran-art-scene-sanctions-1575094.

Rohter, Larry. "An Iranian Storyteller's Personal Revolution." *The New York Times*, July 1, 2012, sec. Books. https://www.nytimes.com/2012/07/02/books/the-colonel-by-the-iranian-writer-mahmoud-dowlatabadi.html.

Sarhangi, Reza. "Persian Arts: A Brief Study." Visual Mathematics. Accessed October 23, 2020. https://www.mi.sanu.ac.rs/vismath/reza1/index.html.

Sinaiee, Maryam. "Underground Designers Thriving In Iran's Fashion Market, Official Admits." Radio Farda, February 1, 2020. https://en.radiofarda.com/a/underground-designers-thriving-in-iran-s-fashion-market-official-admits/30411917.html.

Slavin, Barbara. "Iran Holds First Ever Fashion Week." Al-Monitor, March 27, 2015. https://www.al-monitor.com/pulse/originals/2015/03/iran-fashion-design-trend-clothing-hijab-women-men-west.html.

Suyker, Jeremy. "Iran's Underground Art Scene." Maptia. Accessed October 23, 2020. https://maptia.com/jeremysuyker/stories/iran-s-underground-art-scene.

Tehran Times. "Shahram Mokri: Iran Sanctions Big Obstacle to Joint Film Projects," September 8, 2020. https://www.tehrantimes.com/news/452211/Shahram-Mokri-Iran-sanctions-big-obstacle-to-joint-film-projects.

Vivarelli, Nick. "U.S. Pressure, Sanctions on Iran Take Toll on Its Film Industry." Variety, May 19, 2019. https://variety.com/2019/film/news/trump-pressure-iran-toll-film-industry-1203220112/.

Conclusion

Benjamin, Madea and Sussan Tahmasebi. "Iranian Women Squeezed by US Sanctions, COVID-19 and their Government." Common Dreams. Published on May 14,2020. https://www.commondreams.org/views/2020/05/14/iranian-women-squeezed-us-sanctions-covid-19-and-their-government.

FEMENA. "FEMENA Home Page." Accessed October 23, 2020. https://femena.net/.

Norwegian Refugee Council. "NRC in Iran." Accessed October 22, 2020. https://www.nrc.no/countries/middle-east/iran/.

Thornton, Christopher. "The Iran We Don't See: A Tour of the Country Where People Love Americans." *The Atlantic,* June 6, 2012. https://www.theatlantic.com/international/archive/2012/06/the-iran-we-dont-see-a-tour-of-the-country-where-people-love-americans/258166/.

Made in the USA
Monee, IL
27 April 2021

67080473R00125